4th DIMENSIONAL LIVING

in a

3 DIMENSIONAL WORLD

4th DIMENSIONAL LIVING

in a

3 DIMENSIONAL WORLD

Dr. David Yong-Gi Cho

Institute for Church Growth
Seoul, South Korea

Bridge-Logos
Newberry, Florida 32669

Bridge-Logos

Newberry, Florida 32669 USA

Fourth Dimensional Living in a Three Dimensional World
by Dr. David Yong-Gi Cho

Copyright ©2006 by Bridge-Logos
Reprint 2019

Library of Congress Catalog Card Number: 2006938551
International Standard Book Number: 978-088270-312-1
International Standard Book Number Hardcover: 978-1-61036-227-6
International Standard Book Number Large Print: 978-1-61036-239-9

Contents

CHAPTER 1

Your Invitation to a Fourth-Dimensional World

While living in the three-dimensional realm, you can experience spirituality in the fourth-dimensional realm by faith, as God declares: "Now faith is the substance of things hoped for, the evidence of things not seen. For by it the elders obtained a good testimony. By faith we understand that the worlds were framed by the word of God, so that *the things which are seen were not made of things which are visible*" (Heb. 11:1-3, NKJV, italics mine).

I once had the opportunity to lecture on the topic of church growth at the prominent Fuller Theological Seminary in America. It was quite a gathering; faculty and students of the seminary attended along with leaders of various ministries and organizations throughout America. At the event, I met Dr. Peter Wagner for the first time. He is the one who invited me to come and speak. After we greeted each other, he shared with me a very interesting story. He told me that God had blessed him with a special gift of healing people with deformed legs. He would pray for these people and their legs would grow back to their normal size and length.

I became a little suspicious regarding what I was hearing. Dr. Wagner was a professor and a theologian, and he just didn't look like someone who was capable of carrying out such miraculous healings. My doubtful look must have bothered him, for he invited me to come and see a healing for myself.

So two days later I stopped by his office. What timing! At the office there was an Iraqi whose leg had been amputated as the result of an accident, Mrs. Wagner, Rev. Yongil Kim, and other pastors. Finally, Dr. Wagner walked into the office. After a brief prayer, he laid his hands on the man's leg and shouted, "In the name of Jesus of Nazareth, leg, grow! Leg, grow out! In the name of Jesus of Nazareth, leg, grow!"

He prayed like that for over five minutes. Drenched in sweat, Dr. Wagner shouted these commands over and over again. But the man's leg remained unchanged. At that point, I consoled Dr. Wagner, for I was afraid he might "lose face" if the healing didn't happen.

I said, "I'm sure this man's leg can grow out this instant, but the healing might occur gradually as well."

Everyone in the office said something similar in an effort to console Dr. Wagner. However, he didn't give up. He extended his arms toward the the Iraqi man and directed him to repeat the following prayer after him: "We believe you are a living God. We believe in Jesus Christ, our Lord and Savior. We believe Jesus will heal us surely." Dr. Wagner then asked the man to sit down.

By this time I was beginning to feel awkward and uncomfortable, so I began praying for both Dr. Wagner and the Iraqi man: "Father God, forgive us for our weak faith. Father, whether the leg grows out or not, may Dr. Wagner not miss his footing and lose heart."

Next, Dr. Wagner walked over to the man, placed his hands on his leg, and commanded: "I command in the name of Jesus of Nazareth, leg, grow! Grow out in the name of Jesus of Nazareth!"

Right at that moment, something unbelievable occurred. In fact, I couldn't believe my eyes! I was so stunned that I almost fell backwards. Within thirty seconds, the man's leg grew out!

I was absolutely astounded by the obvious miracle that I had witnessed. I had no idea that God would do something that amazing for us. From that time on I knew quite poignantly how close God really is to our lives. This wonderful healing took place in the office of a professor, not in some church, not on Prayer Mountain, and not in a revival meeting or healing crusade. In strong faith Dr. Wagner simply said, "Grow out, leg!" The Iraqi man walked around the office in utter amazement, and he did not limp or falter as he walked.

How great and awesome God's grace is! He is not far from us. Some may think He's trillions of light-years away from us, but they're so wrong, for He is right here with us, closer than the air we breathe! He hears our words and sees our actions. To this day, our wonderful God is performing miracles through us, the same kinds of miracles that He carried out through Jesus Christ in the Judean hills 2000 years ago.

Dr. Wagner came up to me while I was thanking God for revealing these glorious truths to me. He said, "Dr. Cho, I'm greatly indebted to you for being able to carry out miraculous healings."

I couldn't believe what I was hearing. I tried to argue with him as to how something like this could be credited to me.

Dr. Wagner explained: "Dr. Cho, I read your book, *The Fourth Dimension,* which says that in order to experience God's working, one needs first to dream and then he or she can command the miracle to happen. As we do these things, the miracle we seek shall come to pass. In the office, I firmly believed that the man's leg would be healed and so I proclaimed it with my words. Then I dreamed that I had already seen the healing unfold before my eyes. As a result, the dream really did come to pass."

Because he carried out his work in unwavering faith, he experienced a miracle that I, who had written about such miracles, had never experienced. Dr. Wagner was experiencing a life full of grace and blessing. That was a major wake-up call for me. Through that incident I learned how close God really is to us, and I discovered that through strong, unwavering faith, anything is possible, no matter how great the miracle might seem to be.

I wrote the book, *The Fourth Dimension,* twenty-five years ago. It was about the secrets of the fourth-dimensional world. Actually, learning the spiritual aspects of the fourth-dimensional world and putting the principle of gleaned insights from that world to use as a driving force in my life and ministry were not my own doing or something I learned from another human being. It was the Holy Spirit who taught me these secrets during my long years of fellowship with Him.

But recently, God has been giving new revelations to me on an almost continual basis. Sometimes He does this for more than an hour at a time. During these special encounters, I can hear God's voice speaking repeatedly in the privacy of my own prayer room. His revelations are always deeply moving, and sometimes they "explode" within my inner being, my spirit. This is one of the reasons I've written this new book about the fourth dimension; I want to share God's powerful and awesome revelations with you.

The Bible teaches that things which are seen were not made of things which are visible. (See Heb. 11:3.) What we actually see in the three-dimensional world didn't come into existence through some process of evolution. Darwin's Theory of Evolution claims that the three-dimensional world has evolved by itself and will continue to evolve on its own. But the Bible says that the visible, three-dimensional world didn't just evolve on its own. Instead, the world is influenced and formed by an invisible world that transcends the three-dimensional world.

Therefore, the things which are seen were not made of things which are visible. Some scientific theories say, "What one sees is complete in how it appears." But the Bible says otherwise. The three-dimensional world that is evident to our physical senses doesn't just rely on its own principles to evolve and to form itself.

My special times with God as my Tutor have taught me so many things. How I thank Him for the insights and revelations He has brought to me. His teaching has brought me closer and closer to Him and has drawn me deeper and deeper into an understanding of His awesome creation!

The Secret of the Invisible Fourth-Dimensional World

I felt a strong inspiration from the Holy Spirit deep within my heart one day while I was earnestly praying. In the secret chamber of my heart, I heard a voice speaking to me: *"Pastor Cho, what is one dimension?"*

"It's a line between two points," I said.

I could sense God smiling as He said, *"No, you're wrong."*

"No? One dimension isn't a line?" I responded.

"That's right. Sure, there is a line in one dimension, but it must not have any depth or width to it. Because one dimension doesn't have any thickness or width to it, the line is imaginary."

"I see ..."

His explanation was crystal-clear to me. If a line is drawn with a pencil, that line takes on thickness from the lead. This means that the minute a line is drawn, the line isn't one-dimensional any longer. The line now has depth, which means it is two-dimensional, so to speak. To the extent the line is drawn, it has now become a flat plane. That means that one dimension must not have any depth or space but remain a line, so the conceptual, one-dimensional line is purely imaginary at its core.

Therefore, the one-dimensional figure that we draw to represent something enters the two-dimensional realm and is ruled by that dimension. But if one looks at that illustration from the one-dimensional point of view, one understands that the one dimension has the two-dimensional realm embedded within it.

Let me give you another illustration of this same principle. A plane is two-dimensional, but the minute we draw it, the line takes on depth so, mathematically speaking, it is two-dimensional; but in actuality, it becomes a three-dimensional solid. Of course, one must view it under a microscope to look at these fine details.

Like the one dimension we discussed earlier, the two-dimensional plane, in actuality, is an imaginary plane; a plane that has no thickness whatsoever is two-dimensional. That, too, is imaginary. This means that two-dimensional space, by fate, becomes part of a three-dimensional realm and is controlled by it. From the two-dimensional standpoint, therefore, a two-dimensional realm has the three-dimensional realm embedded within it.

Likewise, the three-dimensional realm, a physical body, includes both time and space in its continuum. Once those two elements came into being, the element of space already belonged to infinity, and the element of time, likewise, became part of infinity. In other words, space is part of infinity, but that space now includes the infinity that is within it.

Similarly, time belongs to eternity, but time also includes eternity. Infinity is embedded in space, and time is embedded in eternity. On that premise, we can say that the fourth-dimensional realm is both a time-space realm, a three-dimensional realm with the element of time added to it. It is a spiritual realm, a world of spirit, a world that completely transcends the physical world.

God is the owner of eternity and infinity. God is eternal and infinite. The Holy Spirit made that point explicitly clear to me in order for me to understand these concepts more clearly.

He said, "*I am not trillions and billions of light-years away. You believe that I'm incapable of understanding what you secretly talk about and your daily life affairs. But you couldn't be more wrong. I am closer than the very heart that pumps inside your chest cavity.*"

Humans are three-dimensional beings. Because humans are part of the three-dimensional realm, once the three-dimensional realm came into being, it became part of the fourth-dimensional realm and is, therefore, under its rule.

When the three-dimensional realm was created, it became susceptible to infinity; and when time came into existence, because it also is part of the three-dimensional realm, we became susceptible to eternity. This principle applies to all humans whether they are Christians or non-believers. We, the three-dimensional beings, were created as beings that are under infinity and eternity.

Therefore, whether we are sitting, standing, sleeping, or awake, we are under God's rule. This is an important beginning to the understanding of God being in our lives. The law of the higher dimension ruling over the lower dimensions is scientifically logical. The first dimension is under the control of the second dimension; the second dimension is under the control of the third dimension; and the third dimension is under the control of the fourth dimension. That is why God, who is eternal and infinite and who lives in the fourth dimension, can rule everything that is under the three-dimensional world in which we live.

The Three-Dimensional World was Created by the God of the Fourth Dimension

The Bible tells us that God is in all creation, and He transcends all. We can interpret this truth in light of our understanding of the different dimensions. The fourth dimension transcends the third dimension even though they belong to each other; the third dimension transcends the second dimension even though they belong to each other; and the second dimension is over the first dimension even though it is part of it. Even though the fourth dimension is susceptible to time and space, it transcends them both.

This means that the fourth-dimensional realm is the spiritual world. The book of Genesis records that the Earth was without form and void; and it tells us that darkness was on the face of the deep. (See Gen. 1:2.) This means that this created world is three-dimensional. Notice how the Holy Spirit hovered over creation like a hen hovers over her eggs.

The Holy Spirit is a Person, a member of the infinite and eternal Godhead. When the Holy Spirit began hovering over the world, His creative work over the three-dimensional world began.

God said, "Let there be light" (Gen. 1:3, NKJV).

Immediately, light came into being. Light was created out of the void; it didn't evolve from something that had existed before.

God then said, "Let there be a firmament in the midst of the waters, and let it divide the waters from the waters" (Gen. 1:6, NKJV).

Thereby the firmament came into being. God called the firmament "Heaven." Even in the creation of the firmament, God created something beautiful from nothingness, and not from something that had existed before. Therefore, we can see that the three-dimensional world did not evolve. The Holy Spirit who belongs to the fourth-dimensional realm personally created it.

The fourth-dimensional world is spiritual. Humans belong to the fourth-dimensional world even though they exist in the three-dimensional world, because they are beings that have both souls and spirits. The spirit of human beings is not equal to that of God, but because we were made in the image of God, we are capable of knowing eternity and infinity. The flesh of men and women returns to dirt, but our spirits either go to Heaven or to hell, and we will forever exist in either of these two places.

From the fourth-dimensional standpoint, human beings are entities that will live forever. The human spirit rules over the flesh that comes from the three-dimensional world. If the spirit grieves, then the flesh becomes ill; when the spirit is sound, then the flesh is healthy. The spirit, even though it resides in the flesh, does not succumb to its rule, but transcends it.

The apostle John ascended into Heaven and saw the glory of God. This experience transcended his flesh even though his body was clearly on the Isle of Patmos. He recorded what he saw in the book of the Revelation. Animals cannot transcend their flesh, or think or speak for that matter. That is because they don't have a spirit.

Isn't that amazing? Because the spirit belongs to the fourth-dimensional realm, it transcends the three-dimensional world.

We reside in our flesh, but if our three-dimensional bodies die, our spirits aren't affected by death. The spirit transcends the three-dimensional realm; therefore, it goes directly to our Lord upon death.

Humans of the Three-Dimensional Realm are Besieged by the Fourth-Dimensional Realm

Colossians 1:13 says, "He has delivered us from the power of darkness and conveyed us into the kingdom of the Son of His love" (NKJV). This verse explains that when we were saved, we were rescued from Satan's fourth-dimensional realm and were delivered into the holy realm where God is.

God brought us out of the power of darkness and transferred us into the good kingdom of the Son of His love. In other words, the beings that belong to the fourth-dimensional realm are God, humans, and Satan. Currently, in the same fourth-dimensional realm, humans occupy the lowest level. Satan is in the middle level, and God is at the highest level. The fourth-dimensional realm occupies the three-dimensional realm; because of this, humans rule over the three-dimensional realm. Also, because humans are spiritual beings, they can bring change to the three-dimensional realm through creating and inventing.

Satan, too, belongs to the fourth-dimensional realm. That is why he tries to control the three-dimensional realm and human beings within the lower realm. Through humans he rules over the third-dimensional realm, and he carries out all sorts of evil deeds within that realm. When we look at the history of civilization, there have been many figures that were given over to evil, including dictators, who have led their civilizations to ruin. Under the control of Satan, they carried out horrendously evil deeds because their spirits and thoughts were under the control of the evil one.

Satan, who took control of Germany's Hitler, for example, led the Nazi leader to cause the genocide of over six million Jews and the spread of destruction and terror throughout Europe. Hitler was eventually driven into the corner of defeat, where he eventually committed suicide. Likewise, Satan entered the emperor of imperialistic Japan. Through him the evil one initiated many wars and spilled the blood of thousands in his attempt to devour the Asian continent.

That's not all. Satan entered Judas Iscariot and influenced him to sell Jesus, the Son of God, for thirty silver coins. If one does not place himself or herself in God, he or she places himself or herself under the influence of the evil side of the fourth-dimensional realm.

Those who accept Christ as their Savior, however, enter into God's eternal, fourth-dimensional realm after being rescued from the part of the fourth-dimensional realm that is governed by humans and Satan. These believers have been rescued by the precious blood of Jesus Christ. Those who are saved are granted eternal life through God's fourth-dimensional realm. And our spirit, heart, and thoughts are completely filled with God's fourth-dimensional realm.

Moving and Using the Spiritual Forces of the Fourth-Dimensional Realm

What are we, who were moved to the holy, spiritual realm by believing in Jesus Christ, supposed to do? We must now think about how we can bear good works and how we ought to live through this fourth-dimensional realm.

The three-dimensional realm is dependent upon how the fourth-dimensional realm operates. The spiritual realm dominates the physical world. The things which are seen were not made of things which are visible. Those who are saved by accepting Christ are led by God from the moment they are born again. The Holy Spirit comes into the three-dimensional realm of believers and fills up their spirits. That's why they are always under the influence of God. It is for that reason that we cannot live by ourselves and unto ourselves any longer.

Because God dwells in us, whenever we watch pornographic magazines or media, we are viewing these things with God. Whenever we try to steal or cheat someone, we do it with God. So how can we stand to do such things? How does doing these things affect the God who dwells within us?

Remember, God is already inside the three-dimensional realm. That is how He extends eternity and infinity to us. From God we obtain the ability to rule the three-dimensional realm. That ability is realized in and through our dreams. The one who dreams can change the three-dimensional world. This does not require someone who studies well or is smart. God wants us to dream and He wants our dreams to be fulfilled. This brings glory to Him as we more fully enjoy the already blessed life God has ordained for us. Therefore, I urge you to fill up your thoughts, heart, and behavior with God's fourth-dimensional realm. Then you will experience a brand-new life that you have never experienced before.

Your Invitation to Operate in the Fourth-Dimensional Realm

Four Elements of Change

What do you suppose one will need in order to operate in the fourth-dimensional world? In order to move the fourth-dimensional world, four elements are required: *Thinking, Faith, Dreaming, and Words.* Our lives will change once we accurately know how these elements work and when we have a proper handle on them. Prayer by itself isn't sufficient. Certainly we need prayer; but first, change must be brought to the invisible fourth-dimensional realm before changes can occur in the visible, third-dimensional realm.

The first dimension, as we said before, is embedded within the second dimension; the second dimension is embedded in the third; and the third is embedded in the fourth. Therefore, in order to change the one-dimensional realm, the two-dimensional realm must be changed; and, likewise, to change the two-dimensional realm, the third-dimensional realm must be changed. This means that ultimately the fourth-dimensional realm must be changed before any changes can take place within the third-dimensional realm.

Now, the changes that are desired in the fourth-dimensional realm depend entirely on what one does with his or her thinking, faith, dreaming, and words – the four critical elements that are needed to realize these vital changes. Only through these means can our lives be changed. How then can we change these elements?

The First Element: Thinking

God gave us the ability to think so that we may bring changes to the fourth-dimensional realm. We cannot account for thinking in three-dimensional terms. Thinking only occurs in the fourth-dimensional realm. Thinking doesn't have thickness or width, and it isn't visible. Thinking is eternal and infinite. Therefore, it's part of the fourth dimension.

Man's imagination is also part of the fourth-dimensional realm. Changes within one's thoughts are reflected in the three-dimensional realm. The Bible, as we pointed out before, tells us that things we see are not made from visible things. A person whose thinking, which is part of the fourth-dimensional realm, is negative will be met with misfortunes in the third-dimensional realm. If the thoughts within his head are: "I'm not qualified," or "I can't do it," or "I'm miserable and sad," then those thoughts will ultimately become manifest in his or her actions in the third-dimensional world. These thought-manifestations will take place in their bodies, finances, work places, etc. Through thoughts—a driving force in the fourth-dimensional realm—everything in the human body and the world comes to pass.

Consequently, an optimist experiences an unfolding of events in his three-dimensional realm with positive outcomes. Such thoughts as these: "I'm healthy," "I'm well-established," and "I'm happy and well" will have tremendous effects in his or her three-dimensional realm.

For instance, if I willfully decide to hold a grudge against someone, I am programing my mind with hateful thoughts, which will have direct consequences with regard to my actions toward the other person in the three-dimensional

15

realm. If I hate another being, I will get hurt first. That's why Jesus tells us to love our enemies. Through loving, forgiving, and praying for our enemies, we may well be doing more good for ourselves than for them.

Despising my enemy calls forth destruction in my own three-dimensional realm. The Bible teaches that a person consists of what he or she thinks about. (See Prov. 23:7). If I think bad thoughts and wish for another's ruin, then my ill intentions will get recorded in my three-dimensional realm and will gradually lead me to receive what I wish for the other person. That's why I say that when I contemplate an evil thought, that evil thought will affect me before it will affect the other person.

It is important for us to know what we're thinking. If we constantly slander and speak ill of others, then such thoughts get recorded within us, and all those evil thoughts will be summoned to destroy ourselves in our three-dimensional world. We often feel badly in our body and mind after we speak of others' flaws and ridicule them in our cliques. That is because those very evil and negative thoughts that we have voiced soon travel directly to our three-dimensional realm.

In the fourth-dimensional realm, there is no You-and-I distinction. There exist only messages. If a message gets recorded in thought within the fourth-dimensional realm, it exerts influence first over our bodies and our daily living. Therefore, there are no secrets. Everything appears in its barest form before God within the fourth-dimensional realm.

If, for some reason, we take on some negative thought, we need to be cured through the Word of God, both the Old Testament and the New Testament. God's Word is part of the fourth-dimensional realm, and it is spirit and life. (See John 6:63). His Word has the ability to correct people's thoughts, to transform their minds, and to change their attitudes. Our three-dimensional realm experiences great change when our thoughts and lives are transformed by the Word of God.

During my forty-seven-year-long ministry, I have never once thought, "My ministry isn't doing well." To the contrary, I always thought, "The ministry is doing well." I would tell myself, "The membership of the congregation is increasing," and "Miracles do occur." As a result, my positive thoughts from the fourth-dimensional realm transferred over to the three-dimensional realm. That is why my ministry always grew; it grew according to how my heart desired it in faith.

Jesus said, "According to your faith let it be to you" (Matt. 9:29, NKJV). Because this is true, I was able to reap results according to my faith. Everything I thought unfolded accordingly in my three-dimensional realm.

Each believer must change his or her thinking according to God's Word; in so doing he or she is thinking according to the fourth-dimensional realm, which is revealed in the Bible. As this happens, God's creative work and manifestations shall come to pass in our lives.

The Second Element: Faith

The second element that can bring about change in our fourth-dimensional realm is *faith*. Faith is a source of powerful strength that can be utilized to bring about a complete change in our three-dimensional realm through the fourth-dimensional realm. The Scripture says, "According to your faith let it be to you" (Matt. 9:29, NKJV), and "If you can believe, all things are possible to him who believes" (Mark 9:23, NKJV).

And Jesus said, "If you have faith as a mustard seed, you will say to this mountain, 'Move from here to there,' and it will move" (Matt. 17:20, NKJV). That's because faith belongs to the fourth dimension, but the mountain belongs to the third dimension. No matter how big and powerful something is, if it's in the third-dimensional realm, it can't do anything by itself. The power to move it is embedded in the fourth-dimensional realm; therefore, change must occur there before any change can take place within the three-dimensional realm, which is included in the fourth-dimensional realm.

Jesus, too, carried out all His miracles in the three-dimensional realm from the faith that comes from the fourth-dimensional realm. The Bible says, "Consequently, faith comes from hearing the message, and the message is heard through the word of Christ." (Rom. 10:17, NIV). Even people who are without faith in Christ work with some type of conviction or belief. Conviction falls under the category of faith, but conviction is only three-dimensional faith.

Animals can't believe because they don't have a spirit. Only humans can have faith because they do have spirits. One must have faith in the Holy Spirit before he or she can move the three-dimensional realm. Faith isn't something you can keep or discard; it's an absolute essential. That's why we must always live by faith. And we must confess our faith.

I always "program" myself by confessing my faith no matter what I am doing, whether I'm sitting down or driving or doing something else. For instance, I confess sayings such as the following: "I believe in Jesus Christ, my personal Savior and Lord;" "I received forgiveness through the precious blood of Jesus Christ;" "I believe in the Holy Spirit who sanctifies me;" "I believe I shall be healed from sickness;" "I believe I shall be blessed;" "I believe in the Resurrection and in everlasting life in heaven;" and "I believe I'm a citizen of God." I am always programing myself in faith. I encourage you to do the same. I want you to see how doing this will affect your whole life. Your life will surely change when you program yourself in faith.

The Third Element: Dreaming

Another element that plays a role in your programing in the fourth-dimensional realm is *dreaming*. God tells us that those who do not dream shall perish. (See Prov. 29:18). We need to dream the dreams of God, which come from the fourth dimension. This gives hope to us in the third-dimensional realm.

Even when we look at non-believers, we often see that it is those who have dreams that bring changes to the world. Now, if believers would only dream in God, who is in absolute control and has dominion over dreams, then our dreams would be more powerful. If we dream the kinds of dreams that God has in store for us, then nothing from the world can stop us from moving the world around us. Therein lies an important point that we need to take note of. The kinds of dreams we dream in God are very different than the dreams that consist of personal ambitions or selfish greed, which are influenced greatly by Satan. We must learn to distinguish between the two types of dreams.

From his childhood on Napoleon dreamed of unifying Europe, which had been segregated for so long. As a result, he ultimately caused quite a commotion in Europe and brought about many changes. Hitler, likewise, dreamed of conquering the entire continent of Europe with his "Aryan race."

Such dreams are rooted in ambition. The people of Europe had to pay the dear price of bloodshed for Hitler's ambitions, which ultimately devastated Europe. Marx and Lenin dreamed of turning the entire world into a system of communism. Their ambitions perished ultimately, but not before starting numerous ethnic conflicts in the three-dimensional realm of eastern Europe, Asia, and Africa.

Weak dreams are no match for powerful dreams. It's important to know that Satan's dreams are much more powerful than those of a human. But God's dreams are much more powerful than those of Satan or those of human beings. Therefore, we must strive to dream dreams that God desires for us to dream through the help of the Holy Spirit. It is the Holy Spirit who allows us to dream. We must program our hearts with dreams that are holy and sanctified by the Holy Spirit.

We can gain good insights into someone's future by noting the kinds of dreams he or she dreams and shares with others. In light of this, I constantly stress the importance of what I call the "Fivefold Gospel and Threefold Blessing" principle. Through it, one can learn to cultivate his or her dreams through the cross. In this way we cultivate dreams that prosper in all things as our soul prospers.

The Fivefold Gospel involves repentance, faith, confession, regeneration, and salvation. The power of the Holy Spirit is active in each of these elements, and He enables us to walk in newness of life, to be filled with His presence, and to experience wholeness of mind, body, and spirit. He comes to dwell within us (see Rom. 8:11); He frees us from the law of sin and death (see Rom. 8:1-2); He enables us to become the children of God (see John 1:12); and through Him we are able to enjoy the blessings God has prepared for us. (See 3 John 2.)

As we apply the Fivefold Gospel to our lives by faith, we are able to experience what I call the Threefold Blessing. It is a blessing for our bodies, souls, and spirits. It is a blessing of wholeness and completion in Christ.

The reason Jesus went through all the persecution, suffering, torture, and anguish that culminated in His death on the cross was to redeem us from all our sins and iniquities. When He cried, "It is finished," He carried upon himself all of our past, present, and future sins. This enabled us to be cleansed and to become righteous before God.

The Son of God, who is the source of all our blessings, destroyed the forces of condemnation through the shedding of His blood, and we have been cleansed and forgiven. He has removed all hatred, anxiety, nervousness, fear, disappointment, and death from us because He loves us. As a result of His death on the cross, we can now experience His supernatural peace and His abundance in every area of our lives, and we can walk in divine health and the assurance that we will live forever with Him.

No matter how difficult your circumstances might be right now, if you will dream fourth-dimensional dreams in your heart, your dreams will seize the three-dimensional realm and change it. Fourth-dimensional dreams are incubated in the three-dimensional realm. No matter how chaotic or empty one's life might be, if he or she will fill his or her life with proper dreams, changes will surely follow—from death to life, from chaos to order, from darkness to light, and from poverty to prosperity. Remember, those changes come from the fourth-dimensional realm.

We often pray diligently in order to find fulfillment for our dreams. When you are in prayer, you should activate the "program" that moves your fourth-dimensional realm. And in order to make your dreams clear and definite, be sure to fast while you pray. By so doing you are able to clear up the fourth-dimensional realm. If you think you can move God's heart by fasting alone, however, you are wrong. Fasting is done first in order to change oneself. In the process, your fourth-dimensional realm will change along with your three-dimensional realm. As this happens, God will now be able to work through you. In other words, God begins working as we allow our body, soul, and spirit to change. So, fast, pray, and give all you've got. Then you'll see that your dreams will no longer remain simply dreams, but they will become reality in your life.

The Fourth Element: Words

Through words we are able to express ourselves, and this is an ability that is exclusive to humans. Humans started and developed their civilization and culture through words. Animals, no matter how ferocious or strong they may be, do not plan, start, or cultivate civilizations. That's because they lack a very basic element that is needed—the fourth-dimensional element of words. Animals do not use language.

The Bible says, "... you have been trapped by what you said, ensnared by the words of your mouth" (Prov. 6:2, NIV)," and,"Death and life are in the power of the tongue, and those who love it will eat its fruit" (Prov. 18:21, NKJV).

Matters of life and death are three-dimensional, but our tongue is of the fourth dimension. The above scriptural passages allude to how powerful one's words actually are. Successful people usually know to be careful with their words. The kinds of words they utter reflect the conditions within their three-dimensional realm. Successful people often claim that what they hope and dream for has already been fulfilled. But unsuccessful people fail already in the kinds of words they choose to use and speak.

The Bible teaches us to profess our dreams and desires in words. That is why our ears and hearts must be exposed often to the Word of God. We need to proclaim the truth of the Scriptures and the promises of God with our voice, speaking their words of truth and life wherever we go. It is worthless for one to wish for success in his third-dimensional realm when he or she has already spoken words of failure in the fourth-dimensional realm.

Jesus said, "I tell you the truth, whatever you bind on earth will be bound in heaven, and whatever you loose on earth will be loosed in heaven" (Matt. 18:18, NIV). This means that everything is either bound or loosed through our words. Negative words lead to bad programing of one's fourth-dimensional realm. When one slanders or speaks ill of others, he or she is programing his or her fourth-dimensional realm with negative words, and these words will end up becoming a curse in his or her three-dimensional realm. Obviously, therefore, a great deal hinges on what comes out of our mouths.

How do we change the words we utter? God made it possible for us to change the words we speak through His Word, which is life and spirit. When we read the Scriptures, we need to memorize and recite them. In this way we are programing our fourth-dimensional realm. When pastors proclaim God's Word from their pulpits, the results are powerful, for they rattle their listeners' fourth-dimensional realm in the process. That is why, when people live obedient and faithful lives before God according to His Word, their entire lives experience a complete change. This is a miraculous work of God. It's never too late for you to begin to effect these changes in your life through God's Word. I challenge you, therefore, to bring your words in line with God's Word.

How is Your Fourth-Dimensional Spiritual World?

Satan has taken over today's world completely. The private lives of people, society in general, and the family in particular are under his sway. We live in a world of darkness, and this makes living in this world feel hollow to most. What should we do about this? We ought to incubate our surrounding environment with fourth-dimensional thinking through faith, dreaming, and our words. Then everything will change. We need to thoroughly examine what we say, think, believe, and dream. And we must realize that such things are of the fourth-dimensional realm, which seriously shakes and rattles our three-dimensional realm.

In order for our lives, businesses, and ministries to succeed, we need to diagnose and pinpoint what elements of our fourth-dimensional realm must be changed so that our three-dimensional realm will move accordingly. This will enable our plans to be fulfilled, and then we will realize success in our endeavors. Depending on our situation, we need to know what element of our fourth-dimensional realm needs to be changed. Do we need to change our thinking, our dreaming, our words, or all three? Once we identify our weak element(s), we can then nourish it/them with God's Word and the power of the Holy Spirit and prayer. As we do so, our three-dimensional lives will experience phenomenal changes.

God revealed His fourth-dimensional spiritual realm to me and led me to write a book about it. It was first written in English, and people from the Americas, Europe, and Africa read that book and experienced remarkable changes in their lives.

This new book, *Fourth-Dimensional Spirituality in a Three-Dimensional World*, was written to provide the reader with an easier understanding of the fourth-dimensional realm and to offer practical guidelines to enable them to apply these principles in their lives. I may not know much about geometry or mathematics, but I have learned and discovered that the concept of one dimension is imaginary, and by fate it has come under the rule of the two-dimensional realm. Once the two-dimensional realm came into being, it became dominated by the three-dimensional realm, and the three-dimensional realm is subsequently governed by the fourth-dimensional realm. When humans are born, whether they like it or not, they are governed by God, who rules the fourth dimension. That's why we must do everything for God.

Without knowing this important truth, believers in Christ will frequently take on foolish thoughts. For example, they may think that God is greatly distant from them. We must believe that our prayers are not prayed in vain and that they are all lifted up to God. We must likewise believe that they will be answered in due time. People who are saved come directly under the control of the Holy Spirit, and in Him are full of the gospel of Christ and all His blessings. A person who knows, believes, dreams, and speaks these facts will experience the blessings of God on a daily basis. He or she will know that all things in his or her life will prosper as his or her soul prospers. (See 3 John 2). This is something God has already promised to us; it is a solid fact of our faith.

The reason we can't dwell in God's promises, even though we have faith in Him, is because we fail to program our fourth-dimensional realm properly. We need to make our fourth-dimensional program—to think, believe, dream, and speak according to the Scriptures—the focus of our daily living. Then we shall experience God's wonderful works in our lives.

Our prayers need fourth-dimensional programing in order for their power to become manifest. Praying is the work of lifting up newly programed elements of the fourth-dimension into God's kingdom. After we reprogram our fourth-dimensional realm and pray to God, He will carry out His promises according to our faith. The Scripture reveals to us that this will happen through our thinking, our faith, our dreams, and our words. The responsibility is ours. Therefore, it is vitally important for us to program our fourth-dimensional realm ourselves; God will then carry out His work in our behalf. It should not be surprising that we find the following entreaty in our Lord's Prayer: "Your will be done on earth as it is in heaven" (Matt. 6:10, NKJV). The reason we pray, "And do not lead us into temptation, but deliver us from the evil one"

(Matt. 6:13, NKJV), is so that God's will would be accomplished in our lives and in the world.

God told Adam to "fill the earth and subdue it. Rule over [be masters of] the fish of the sea and the birds of the air and over every living creature that moves on the ground [all the animals]" (Gen. 1:28, NIV). This shows us that we may program our fourth-dimensional realm in such a way that we will be able to rule over all creation.

Psalm 81 says, "Open your mouth wide, and I will fill it" (Ps. 81:10, NKJV). The mouth, as I pointed out earlier, refers here to the fourth dimension. It is God's promise that He will help us in all areas of our lives when we program our fourth-dimensional realm according to His will and His Word.

If we take heed to all these biblical truths about fourth-dimensional spirituality and apply them to our lives, we will definitely experience change. From now on, instead of speaking ill of others or deprecating them in any way, you will fill your mouth with whatever you gather from your fourth-dimensional realm. You will speak words of life and victory without any wrath or doubting. You will become an encourager.

We cannot hide from God. We have been taken over by God's fourth-dimensional realm, and are standing bare before Him. If we program our fourth-dimensional realm well, He will pour out His blessings upon us and through us. It's never too late to begin. Start now with this reprograming. If you do, you will become a new person. You are destined to succeed. If you incorporate the program of the Holy Spirit—which is fully revealed in the Word—into your life, you will experience the marvelous workings of God's creative power. This is a deeply profound truth that God has revealed to me. I sincerely hope you can experience the fourth dimension in your life and let it reach out to your surrounding environment. It's time for you to train your fourth-dimensional thinking, faith, dreams, and words in the Word, prayer, and the Holy Spirit. Already, your life has begun to change!

CHAPTER 2

Thinking

Change Your Thinking to Correspond to the Fourth-Dimensional Realm.

The Bible says, "For to be carnally minded is death, but to be spiritually minded is life and peace" (Rom. 8:6, NKJV).

You can think with your flesh or with your spirit. The Scriptures reveal how important it is for humans to dwell on spiritual thinking rather than "worldly" [*of the flesh*] thinking.

Paul the apostle tells us more about this important subject: "For those who live according to the flesh set their minds on the things of the flesh, but those who live according to the Spirit, the things of the Spirit. For to be carnally minded is death, but to be spiritually minded is life and peace. Because the carnal mind is enmity against God; for it is not subject to the law of God, nor indeed can be" (Rom. 8:5-7, NKJV). This passage serves as a stark reminder to us with regard to how we should be thinking.

To the extent that we mentally map out our plans for success and carry out those plans accordingly, our assurance of success increases. However, if a person is more focused on failure than on success, the likelihood of his or her failure will increase. When our minds dwell upon success, our thinking will yield positive outcomes, and the fulfillment of our dreams will be expedited.

Instead of gradually developing toward a goal, the human psyche tends to make a quantum leap toward something when a certain level of attainment has been reached. Many athletes believed for a long time that human beings could not run a mile in four minutes or less. They used to have a saying, "the four-minute jinx," with regard to this belief. In those days, whenever track-and-field tournaments were held, even world-class runners couldn't complete the mile within four minutes. That was until Roger Bannister came along. He broke through that false barrier in 1954.

Roger Bannister began employing different running styles on his own in order to break the "four-minute jinx." He believed it was possible to run the four-minute mile, and to realize his goal, he spent time changing his running style, and more importantly, his thought patterns. As a result, Roger Bannister became the first man to run a mile within four minutes. Amazingly, after he broke through this barrier and destroyed the jinx, athletes around the world began to run the mile in four minutes or less! Bannister's change in thinking and believing helped to change everyone's thinking about running the mile.

Unlike Bannister, other athletes did not attempt to change their running style and old patterns. What they finally changed, though, as they followed in Bannister's footsteps, was their thinking. They told themselves and proclaimed to others, "I can do it!" Once they started believing that they were able to run faster, their actions followed their thoughts and everything began to change. Once you start believing that something is possible, the likelihood of your taking the action to achieve that goal will greatly increase.

Yes, thinking influences your physical responses. Whenever you watch absorbing movies or read books, newspaper articles, or magazine articles, and imagine something depicted in writing or from an image, your body will react accordingly. Whenever you imagine something that is light and humorous, your body will feel light and energized. Thinking about scary scenes from a horror movie, on the other hand, will cause your heart rate to rise. Similarly, imagining a romantic scene will stir excitement within you.

Athletes, therefore, should train mentally before engaging in physical training. There is a powerful link between thinking and physical responses. Managers and coaches often give inspiring talks, hoping for adrenaline to be released within the bodies of their team members. Shooters and archers utilize thinking to achieve calmness in their hearts and greater confidence within.

Likewise, swimmers and track runners train their minds to imagine themselves in actual matches and competitions. According to research, when athletes engage in such thinking, their bodies actually react to what they see with their mind's eye, and certain muscles constrict as they would during real performances.

Your mental attitude can also have an effect on your health. They say the type of mental attitude a patient takes on after being diagnosed with cancer may help to determine how long he or she will live. For instance, a person who accepts the diagnosis of cancer as a death sentence will immediately cause himself or herself to fall into despair and contemplate death and the funeral ceremony. Consequently, this person will not live as long as another person who thinks more optimistically and remains hopeful.

Thinking is an actual substance that can yield either optimistic results or the opposite. Thinking cannot be seen through physical eyes, but it is an important element of the fourth dimension that determines all aspects of one's life in a three-dimensional world. Therefore, change your thinking and apply it to your life. As you do so, you will experience amazing life-changing results.

Unconditional optimism is humanistic thinking. What we need, instead, is God's thinking. This comes to us as we meditate on the Scriptures. As we converse with God, He will lead us to examine our lives, reflect upon our lives, repent of anything that is contrary to Him, and change our way of thinking.

Thinking influences your feelings and behaviors, as well as your physical body. It is wrong to assume, however, that thinking positively alone will solve all our problems. Such positive thinking may be fourth-dimensional, but it's nevertheless still human thinking. Powerful fourth-dimensional thinking has its foundation in the Holy Spirit, the Word, and prayer.

The Word of God and prayer in the Holy Spirit are powerful means to seek new ways or solutions for dealing with problems, because they show us how to discern three-dimensional circumstances in their positive, negative, or neutral states. That is why we must begin thinking in God's ways, not our own.

The Word possesses amazing power. Through the Word, all creation came into existence, and through the Word all miracles were accomplished. Jesus, too, used the Word to defeat Satan when He encountered him in the wilderness. If we can take the powerful Word of God and permanently focus on it in our thinking and apply it to our lives, we shall experience amazing changes in our lives.

First, you need to have the Word always at your disposal and not just be content with simply reading it. We need to hide the Word in our hearts and have certain verses committed to memory for immediate use in spiritual combat. Nothing is more effective than the Word of God for use in fighting against an evil spirit. Therefore, it is critical to set aside time to memorize the Word so you can apply it to your life. Keep memorizing verses so you can repeat them if necessary, and keep practicing so you won't forget the ones you already know. Through these means you will be able to take the sword of the Spirit by its handle and use it as your weapon of offense and defense.

Next, you must meditate on God's Word. (See Psalm 1:1-2 and Josh. 1:8). Meditating on the Word helps believers to understand the Scriptures and it reminds them to apply it to their daily lives. Do your best to always meditate on the Word. Meditate as you hear, read, study, and memorize the Word. As a result, your faith and thinking will grow and change, your mind will be renewed, and you will be transformed.

I once read a book that was written by Deacon Jung Moonsik, a Sunday school teacher. I was deeply touched by his book. The deacon is currently the president of Yire Electronics, but his initial motive for starting his company was to observe the Lord's Day so he could faithfully serve as a Sunday school teacher. He quit his work at the company that had required him to work on Sundays and started his own business twelve years ago.

The deacon's parents passed away when he was only ten. He went on to finish his high school education by attending night school. After working at a company for three years, he left to start his business in a five-pyeong space (one room) in a basement with only $500.00, his company pension. In his book, he refers to times during those early days when he wanted to end his life because he felt it was too difficult to bear.

One day he heard a preacher say these words: "Don't be misled by lies and meaningless pursuits, but always remain faithful in God as you go forward, not paying attention to your immediate circumstances." These words gave him renewed strength and faith in God, and he used those realizations to overcome the hardships of his life.

The reason he was able to bounce back from a major breakdown, despair, and hardship was because he fed himself properly on spiritual food. He encouraged himself by hearing and meditating on the Word of God. He observed the Lord's Day, served in the Sunday school, and faithfully tithed and gave additional offerings for missions. He even set up a scholarship fund for students who attended the church.

Living a godly and faithful life, he is now the president of a business that brings in millions of dollars in profits. What caused this man to change so drastically? Deacon Jung lived a life not along the lines of his own thinking but according to God's Word. We can glean a valuable lesson from his life. We can receive God's blessings when we conduct our lives according to God's Word. Therefore, I urge you to fill your thinking with God's Word.

Our thinking is like a football that may bounce off in any direction. This can be very treacherous indeed, especially when our thinking, emotions, and wills get mixed together. The only thing that can tame our thinking and help us find a proper path to tread is the Word of God. If our thinking is seized by the Word of God and we begin to pursue a life of obedience to His Word, we then begin to bear fruit for God. This happens as our experiences change in the three-dimensional environment.

Through God's Word we are able to change completely the way we think. That's because God's Word is the living word of God. Hebrews 4:12 says, "For the word of God is living and powerful, and sharper than any two-edged sword, piercing even to the division of soul and spirit, and of joints and marrow, and is a discerner of the thoughts and intents of the heart" (NKJV).

Only through God, who bestows His power upon us, can we overcome all of our circumstances. Paul writes, "I can do all things through Christ who strengthens me" (Phil. 4:13, NKJV). We realize the truth of this verse when we place our total faith in God. Through His Word, our tendency to give up will change radically.

God paid a dear price by sacrificing His Son on the cross, and through the shed blood of Christ He gave us all we need. Therefore, we must never forget that we are able to carry out all things in Christ, who conquered the three-dimensional world. Even when we pass through the gloomy valley of death, as long as we trust that God is with us and that He has placed us safely under His wings, we can have a real, genuine peace. As long as we have the trust in God that He is always with us, our thoughts will change and we will think more optimistically. This will enable us to reel in the strength we need to overcome all despair and hopelessness.

When the way we think changes, we will bear spiritual fruit. This happens because the Word of God opens the door to the fourth dimension for us. This enables God's creative miracles to occur in our lives. Our job is to keep our thoughts and the intentions of our hearts in line with God's Word. As we do so, we will experience victory, and God's kingdom will be fully absorbed in our lives and in our surrounding environment.

Once we accept Jesus Christ, the Holy Spirit takes up His residence in our hearts. He baptizes us, and when we are filled with Him, God's joy will fill up our hearts. When the disciples gathered in Mark's upper room on the Day of Pentecost, the Holy Spirit entered into them, and as a result they all received a fullness of joy that they had never experienced before. From then on, they were recharged with faith for the Lord, and they were filled with the energy of love.

Without joy in our hearts, we have no desire to keep on working for the Lord; consequently, we may give up when difficulties loom in our lives. With our joy gone and our energy running low, we won't be able to accomplish anything. But if we are filled with the Holy Spirit and our hearts are filled with joy, we will become courageous and be able to take on anything that comes our way. Whatever adversities or difficult circumstances life might bring to us, with the infilling of the Holy Spirit we are able to overcome them. In this way we will become vital witnesses in the world.

Peter denied Jesus three times. However, once he was filled with the Holy Spirit, he witnessed to 3,000 people in one day. On the second day he raised the paralyzed man who was sitting at the entrance to the Temple. Peter also brought 5,000 to repentance and led many souls to Jesus, ultimately becoming one of the greatest biblical leaders of all time. Once the Holy Spirit enters our lives, we are no longer afraid to witness for Jesus Christ, no matter what the cost might be. Such strength and courage are not our own, but they come from the working of the Holy Spirit in our lives and through us.

Jesus' disciples consisted of fishermen and tax collectors. Most of them were looked down upon according to the world's standards, but they became filled with the Holy Spirit, and joy filled their hearts. Their thoughts were once filled with all the negativity of the world, but these men were changed into courageous, bold and loyal followers of Jesus Christ, which ultimately led them to witness for Jesus and His gospel throughout Jerusalem, Judea, Samaria, Rome, and to the ends of the earth. (See Acts 1:8).

Once we become filled with the Holy Spirit, our thoughts will become more and more like those of the Holy Spirit. As a result, our thoughts become more positive and creative. Our thinking becomes filled with the belief that anything is possible through faith, and gradually we will become more courageous.

No matter what problems you may be confronted with, change your negative thoughts into positive ones. Like Jesus, who overcame death, you can overcome despair.

During my forty-seven years of pastoral ministry, I have never held any negative thoughts about the ministry. I always thought, "The church will grow and God will send His sheep." Whenever negative or despairing thoughts tried to creep into my mind, I confronted them directly as soon as they appeared. I confessed that in all things God works for the good of those who love him, to those who have been called according to His purpose. (See Rom. 8:28). In this way God was able to change my thoughts into positive ones.

Therefore, the proper message from my fourth-dimensional realm transferred into my three-dimensional realm, which caused deep changes within me and allowed me to carry on a ministry with a powerful impact. As a result, my ministry was carried out according to what God revealed to me in my heart.

SaemauelDuring the Park Jung Hee military regime of the 60's, an economic revitalization movement began to occur in South Korea. Countless people left their hometowns for Seoul. People who came to Seoul without any plans settled into areas like Ahyun-dong and Nhengchun-dong, and they built shacks to live in.

At that time our church called that area "Heaven #1." That's because we knew God would help us the most when we found ourselves in the most desperate circumstances. My ministry partner Choi Ja-sil and I witnessed to the people who were living in the slums. It was then that God initiated a powerful Holy Spirit movement in the Seodae-gate area through our ministry.

I would tell the people, "God baptizes us with the Holy Spirit, allows us to speak in tongues through the Holy Spirit, and permits us the nine spiritual gifts through Him. So accept the Holy Spirit … ."

This was how I witnessed to the people and urged them to be filled with the Holy Spirit and receive His nine spiritual gifts. Moreover, I always stressed to our church members to renew their hearts. Subsequently, the "renewing of the heart" movement began.

One day, President Park Jung Hee summoned me to the Blue House and asked me, "Pastor Cho, do you have any idea how to renew our people and to bring changes to our fishing and agrarian villages?"

I answered him confidently, "President Park, changes can only come about if we change our thinking. Why don't you start a "renewing of the heart" movement to get people to think more optimistically. In many cities, there are churches, so why don't you start the movement using those churches as the center. I'm sure you'll experience a wonderful success."

Right then, President Park called in the Secretary of the Ministry of Home Affairs, Kim Hyun-oak, and said, "Pastor

Cho suggested a 'renewing of the heart' movement. What do you think?"

Then minister Kim responded, "I think it's a great idea. But it has a religious ring to it. Why don't we change the name to "*Saemauel* (literally meaning, *a new village*) movement?"

The president then turned to me for my feedback. I told him that no matter what you call it, unless the hearts of people are changed, nothing will succeed. I also emphasized the need to start the "renewing of the heart" movement first so as to bring changes to the hearts of the people.

Subsequently, however, it was the *Saemauel* movement that spread throughout the nation like wildfire. But at the core of that movement was the idea of changing people's hearts, and it was the renewing of the heart, with churches serving as the center of the movement, that originally gave birth to the *Saemauel* movement.

I proclaimed the message of hope through the "renewing of the heart" movement. The Bible says, "Therefore, if anyone is in Christ, he is a new creation; old things have passed away; behold, all things have become new" (2 Cor. 5:17, NKJV). I proclaimed the powerful message of hope from God to get rid of some of the negative thoughts in the hearts of the church members. I declared confidently and boldly, "Take on the *can-do* spirit; get rid of any negative 'let's give up' thoughts, and believe in God's miracles ...."

In those days, the living circumstances were so dire for many that no one was able to live through human reasoning alone. Often I proclaimed God's truths in the following way: "Believe in miracles. The God who once parted the

Red Sea and who brought down the walls of Jericho is alive and well. Because of Him, we know poverty and hunger will go away, and we shall soon welcome in His blessings. In faith, expect miracles!"

I continued to instruct our church members to confess the Scriptures by mouth, to live their lives in faith, and to dream God's dreams. Again and again, I made them recite certain scriptural passages, such as the following: "I can do all things through Christ who strengthens me" (Phil. 4:13, NKJV); "And we know that all things work together for good to those who love God, to those who are the called according to His purpose" (Rom. 8:28. NKJV); and, "If you can believe, all things are possible to him who believes" (Mark 9:23, NKJV).

The congregation couldn't really adapt well to my style of preaching; nonetheless, I realized what this spiritual feeding was accomplishing for their overall growth. Then, as they experienced the miracles themselves, they began to proclaim the same message to others.

Well-known pastors in Korea and around the world constantly inquire about the phenomenal growth of Yoido Full Gospel Church and its affiliated churches which are led by my protégés. They often say that there must be some "specially kept secret" for growth, so they pressure us to share "the secret" with them. In response to them, I often use an old saying, "Bamboos grow from the bamboo garden." In this way I attempt to explain the principles and the "secrets" of church growth.

41

My pastor-protégés learn from my ministry style at Yoido Full Gospel Church, and this gives them a bigger frame of mind. They learn about the can-do spirit, and we develop visions and pastoring philosophies together. During their training process they take on bigger thoughts and dreams for ministry. Their thinking does not remain static or constant, but it is dynamic. It constantly changes and grows into something else.

These pastors cultivate their thinking until it grows into something larger, and in this way they are able to take on big visions and dreams of big ministries. This is an affirmation of the saying I alluded to earlier about bamboos growing from the bamboo garden. Growth in thinking has its roots deeply planted in maturity; it results in both quality and quantity.

Human thinking has creative power. One's success in ministry cannot be judged solely on the size of a minister's church. Churches in fishing and agrarian villages are part of God's sovereign plan just as are churches in urban areas. The reason I'm talking about size here, though, is in reference to the "size" of one's thinking. In other words, what ultimately happens is related to the "size" of one's thinking. If what one thinks is small, the result will be "small" fruit. On the other hand, big thoughts have the potential to yield "bigger" fruit.

What's more important here, though, is that one must cultivate positive and aggressive fourth-dimensional thinking within the domains of his or her expectations. Just because one thinks big doesn't mean he or she will have bigger fruit. Thinking is only the beginning; there must be corresponding actions which support the thoughts. For instance, a farmer who only thinks and dreams of a big harvest but never does the work of planting the seed, will not reap a harvest. However, if one thinks big, then he or she must be sure to back up the thoughts by planting the seed of action and doing the necessary work.

As I reminisce about my forty-seven years of pastoral ministry, I begin to realize that not only did I think big, but in order to realize such big thoughts and dreams, I had to work diligently and consistently with sacrifice and dedication. In order to realize your thinking in reality, you must pay your dues by giving everything to your God-given goals.

Hebrews 11:3 says, "By faith we understand that the universe was formed at God's command, so that what is seen was not made out of what was visible" (NIV). In other words, the visible, three-dimensional realm is influenced by the fourth-dimensional realm. For example, a negative-minded person whose thinking (a fourth-dimensional element) is negative will only experience negative things in his three-dimensional realm. But someone who thinks clearly and positively will experience good things in life since his or her thinking is good.

Our bodies are a type of "fourth-dimensional computer lab." The thing that turns on the "computer" and creates the programs is our thinking. Thinking creates wavelengths in the fourth-dimensional realm. And such wavelengths influence our three-dimensional realm and offer us the generating power to obtain results in our lives.

The program that was accessed to create our thinking pattern will determine the results that will be achieved. For example, a depressing, negative, and ailing-mind-set program will yield depressing and negative results in our lives and our bodies, elements of the three-dimensional realm. Once our thinking fills up with depressing thoughts and anger, such elements will automatically program our bodies, and this will lead to stress and ultimately to illness.

But someone who relies on a positive mind-set to create his or her thinking program will always experience a good outcome in his or her three-dimensional realm. Such thoughts as "I'm healthy"; "I'm happy"; and "I feel great" will exert tremendous influence over the three-dimensional realm, so the person's life will become filled with vigor and happiness.

Therefore we need to take on a positive, persuasive mind-set. The persuasive mind-set is the "can-do" mind-set. Becoming negative in all things is not healthy. To think negatively, as in the following examples, "I can't do it"; "I'm not good for it"; and "My life is hopeless," is disastrous.

Someone who thinks positively is someone who believes anything is possible. The Scripture says, "If you can believe, all things are possible to him who believes" (Mark 9:23, NKJV). The person with a positive mind-set always has belief in his or her heart. He or she plans and carries out goals with the attitude of "I can do it" and "Let's give it a try," and doesn't think about failure. Always think success and take on the mind-set of not giving up.

Ever since the fall of mankind, humans have been full of negative elements in their thinking. Unless you get rid of negativity, such as anger, hopelessness, and insecurity, those elements will turn back on each other and cause problems in your life.

Depravity-filled human thinking is fundamentally made up of negative elements. That's why negative thinking turns back on other negative thinking, creating problem after problem. There are many destructive elements in human thinking. These elements are found in our small and big "tidal waves" of hatred and anger, fear and insecurity, sadness and hopelessness, and sin and the world.

We must change the things that constitute our thinking in order to live victoriously. To learn what the components in one's thinking are, one should examine the source of his or her thoughts. Since thinking tends to adapt more easily to the elements that feed it, we must allow our minds to be influenced by positive, creative, and productive environments. Therefore it is imperative to fight off anger, fear, and a negative environment, for these elements are counteractive to the fourth-dimensional realm.

Anger that resides in our hearts causes our thinking programs to become negative. Anger creates and begets anger. Proverbs 15:18 says, "A wrathful man stirs up strife, but he who is slow to anger allays contention" (NKJV). Wrath gets in the way of fulfilling God's will. Anger stirs up destructive and "end-of-all-things" sentiments that block us from making the right decisions regarding various matters.

During World War II, the fundamental reason why Hitler was defeated was due to his wrath. Hitler possessed clear thinking, analytic ability, public-speaking acumen, and sharp decision-making and leadership skills. But he was also a wrathful man. A little thing could easily stir up anger within him. His followers knew this about him and were careful not to report anything to him that might arouse his anger. Even when Hitler was up against Great Britain and France in a difficult battle, his sudden temper prompted him to pull out part of his troops in order to attack the Soviet Union, which dealt a fatal blow to his military plans and marked the worst mistake of his lifetime.

When the united Allies were carrying out the invasion of Normandy, all Hitler would have had to do was redirect his troops that were headed toward the Soviet Union back to Normandy in order to hinder the Allies' operations, but his adjutant general was too afraid to wake Hitler up from his nap to let him know about the impending invasion. He knew the type of anger that would befall him if he were to interrupt Hitler's nap. Hitler was known to burst into wrath over trivial matters. Therefore, while Hitler was in a deep sleep, the Allies had already landed in Normandy and secured their position. As a result, the Nazis were eventually defeated. It was Hitler's anger that paved the way for his defeat and the destruction of the Third Reich.

We must overcome all fear of sadness and hopelessness, insecurity, and other thoughts that inject negativity into our hearts. Such things rob us of our hope, life, and vitality, and they invite gloominess into our lives.

1 John 4:18 tells us, "There is no fear in love; but perfect love casts out fear, because fear involves torment. But he who fears has not been made perfect in love" (NKJV). There are always penalties associated with fear. If you are afraid of cancer, the fear of cancer will torment your life. If you are afraid of poverty, the fear of poverty will torment your life. If you are afraid of war, the fear of war will torment your life. Yes, fear is always accompanied by torment.

Fear of sadness robs your heart of hope. Sadness, like the rainy monsoon season, dampens our spirits. Once sadness fills our hearts, our lives will become negative and we will lose our hope. However, our lives are not immune to sadness. Most people look happy on the outside, but often they are weeping in their hearts, where sadness comes down like pouring rain. Sadness is another emotion that changes our thinking into a negative mind-set.

Fear of setbacks and losses in life will change our thinking negatively and cause us to give up easily. The only way we are able to overcome suffering in our lives and bounce back from setbacks is through our trusting in God and placing our hope in Him.

We were born into a negative world. After committing sin against God, humankind was thrown out of Eden. Since then, we've lived in this cursed world, and we can't escape from it. Actually, we have been saturated in negativity from our childhoods on. We grew up hearing negative statements: "You can't do it"; "Don't do it"; "Living is painful"; "I'm suffering," etc. Most of us saw, heard, and spoke negativity. Even in papers and on TV most of what we see, especially the news, is negative. Whether it is something the government has done wrong, the irregularities of politicians, money-laundering and embezzlement in corporations and firms, or crime in its various forms, it's all negative. Even dramas on TV depict stories of couples breaking up, families falling apart, and various other negative themes.

The fact is that we have become so accustomed to negativity that when we actually see or hear something positive for a change, we don't react with rejoicing, because we're expecting only negative things to come forth. On the other hand, when something negative is depicted, we often have immediate reactions, such as crying or expressions of shock. All too frequently people entertain themselves with negative stories. The devil is constantly on the prey, and he tries to influence our lives with negativity. If we let his negativity influence us, we can't live successful and fulfilling lives. Thinking is the vessel through which God carries out His workings. As long as we hold onto negative thoughts, God's workings cannot become manifest in our lives.

Whenever I'm preaching from the pulpit, I always aim to change the church members' fourth-dimensional realm – their spiritual realm. In order to accomplish this I try to help them change their thought patterns. When I'm able to help them fix their fourth-dimensional realms, they will naturally bear positive fruit.

Problems in fourth-dimensional thinking hinder us from seeing life from a positive point of view, and they keep us from using creative thinking and opening our hearts. Almost everyone looks at their incompetence and hopelessness in life; therefore, their "boat of life" sinks. No one in this world is perfect or competent in everything. But those who dwell on their failings and incompetencies will lose their willingness to move; subsequently, they will fall into the pit of hopelessness. Someone who rises above his or her environment by thinking positively, clearly, creatively, and productively will reflect those qualities in the fruit they bear.

There are times when one's view of a situation will differ drastically from the actual situation. The fortress we may see in front of us might be tall, and its inhabitants might look like giant figures when we compare ourselves with them, and this might make us feel like helpless creatures. Similarly, the land might look like a wilderness to us. However, such conditions, as we perceive them, may be very different from what they actually are. The planet we live on—the earth—may look flat to us, as we look out upon the horizon. Even if we take ourselves to the top of a mountain and look out as far as we can see, the earth will still look flat, even at the farthest point. That's why there's an old saying, "Don't go too far from home." In earlier times it was forbidden to sail far into the sea. That's because people held to the idea that the world was flat, and they thought that sailors might fall off the end of the earth if they went too far!

The truth was entirely different from what they imagined. We now know that the earth is round. This is a good example of the truth that what we see and what the reality actually is can be totally different.

Here's another example. The earth does not seem to be spinning on its axis. That's because the world isn't turning in such a way that we can actually feel the movement. We don't seem to be on a spinning planet, but in actuality the earth is rotating on its axis quite rapidly as it revolves around the sun. The fact that we don't see it or feel it does not change this truth. This is why we must let go of our feelings and preconceptions, and think beyond our immediate surroundings and senses in order to experience miracles. Thinking is a fourth-dimensional element that exceeds both the environment and our physical senses.

We can always experience change as we rise above our environment through the cross of Jesus Christ. The cross represents the power that can save the dying and that can cause something to exist out of nothing. In the cross we have the power to change hopelessness to hope. Fourth-dimensional thinking overcomes our immediate environment, as we consider the cross to be the very force that changes our ability to see, understand, and perceive the truth.

You have been blessed. Therefore, you should take on what I call richness of thinking. Fill up the stockroom of your thoughts with the Fivefold Gospel and the blessings of joy.

I always taught my church members to think of the Fivefold Gospel and the Threefold Blessing. The Bible teaches that the things of God should be taught as being pure, good, worthy of compliments, and able to be accomplished. That's why I always think about such things on a daily basis.

For example, I will frequently remind myself, "I've received forgiveness and am now a righteous person. I'm a holy person who is filled with the Holy Spirit. I've been healed. I've been released from the bondage of sin. I am experiencing eternal life and blessings."

In a similar vein, I always remind myself, "All is well, and my body and soul are as healthy as can be!" By so doing, I'm filling up my fourth-dimensional realm completely with victory, success, richness, health, and blessings; and naturally my three-dimensional realm will follow.

You must fill up your thinking with victory, success, and things that are divinely rich. Remember, you already possess those things. (See Eph. 1:3).

During the Korean War, most Korean people lived a life of extreme poverty. At that time, whenever trains would arrive with coal, people would climb to the top of the train cars in their desperate attempts to get [steal] some pieces of coal for themselves. Their actions would prompt soldiers to come after them, so they often had to run away.

I remember one day in my childhood when the train arrived with coal piled high. People swarmed around it like ants searching for food crumbs. One ten-year-old child climbed to the top and threw down some pieces of coal so his father could pick them up. Right then, one huge piece of coal fell and rolled underneath the train. The soldiers saw what was happening and ran toward the train. The boy jumped to the ground but spotted the large coal under the train. He didn't hesitate to crawl underneath to grab it. At that moment, the train began to move.

The people who were witnessing this yelled out. I was one of them. But no one tried to rescue the boy. At that moment, I saw a person quickly rushing toward the moving train. It was the father of the boy. He was barely able to push his son out from under the train, but he couldn't get himself out from under the train car in time. Even today, I get the shivers when I recall that event. I saw what that father did for his son, and I remember how, even when he was being run over by the train, the father waved to his son, directing him to flee to safety. The father was killed in that incident.

I remember wondering, "Why did the father give up his life to save the boy? He could have another son; why did he kill himself?"

51

I was only a middle school student at the time, so I really couldn't understand what it is like to be a parent. Now that I am a father, though, I think I can understand why that father so bravely risked his life. There is no theory or logic behind a father's love for his child. Love is stronger than death, and this is what prompted the father to move swiftly to rescue his son. Love gave him the courage and the willingness to sacrifice his own life for his son. That father could have saved his life and could have survived on his own; but seeing his son in danger, he could not leave his son to die. I'm sure most fathers would act the same way.

Our Father God loves us in the same way. He loves us so dearly that He sacrificed everything to save us. That's why He gave us His Son. God himself took upon himself human flesh in order to die on the cross. Once we realize that God loves us and that He is always with us, then our hearts will be filled with courage. These changes take place in our fourth-dimensional realm. We truly have a solid basis to believe that since God is with us, everything is possible. In light of this, we must live our lives with the thought that "everything is possible," and as we do so, we will experience victory and miracles in our daily lives.

What evidence do we have to support our richness of thinking that tells us we are already blessed with everything? We know it for sure through the death and the resurrection of Jesus Christ. He showed us His love by dying on the cross and giving up everything for us. Therefore, when we cling to the cross, our despair and restlessness, along with death and hell, will disappear, leaving us with God's glory and the resurrection. All that we find in the work of Christ on the cross turns the bitter water of despair and hopelessness into the sweet water of life.

Romans 8:35-39 tells us, "Who shall separate us from the love of Christ? Shall tribulation, or distress, or persecution, or famine, or nakedness, or peril, or sword? As it is written: 'For your sake we are killed all day long; we are accounted as sheep for the slaughter.'Yet in all these things we are more than conquerors through Him who loved us. For I am persuaded that neither death nor life, nor angels nor principalities nor powers, nor things present nor things to come, nor height nor depth, nor any other created thing, shall be able to separate us from the love of God which is in Christ Jesus our Lord" (NKJV). This passage gives us clear evidence that God has turned the sour water of our lives into the sweet-tasting water of life through Jesus Christ.

I have been sharing with you the first element of the fourth-dimensional realm, which is *thinking*. Depending on how we exercise our fourth-dimensional thinking, whether "of the spirit" or "of the flesh," our lives can change for the better or for the worse. First, it's imperative to live a life that is guided and ruled by the Holy Spirit, for the Holy Spirit offers us life and peace. When we are captivated by the Holy Spirit and we learn how to think with Him and like Him, we are able to fulfill our hopes through His working in and through us. Because our thinking influences others, we need to enter into a close, intimate relationship with the Holy Spirit so that His influence will take over our lives.

Second, our thinking is like spiritual breathing; and through our prayers, our thoughts will get expressed to God. Then our thoughts will bear fruit. Prayer provides us with the power to change our fourth-dimensional thinking into reality.

Because God rules over everything, once we let Him take care of our affairs through prayer, He will grant our prayer requests, thereby enabling us to bear fruit. God gave humans a special privilege to interact with Him through prayer. Prayers that are built from God's own will and thoughts will surely yield the power that will move God's heart.

Third, our thinking needs to be captivated by the Word. Only the Scriptures can train our unpredictable thinking and guide us onto the right path. Once our thinking is saturated with the Word and we begin to obey its teachings, we will bear fruit and experience change in our three-dimensional realm.

Now that you know these truths, it's time to change your thinking. When your life is filled with thinking that focuses on God, then your life will experience fullness of joy, and you will shine like the sun, always burning brightly, and this will provide you with joy and hope on a day-to-day basis.

Thinking

CHAPTER 3

Faith

You Can Change the Fourth-Dimensional Spiritual World within You

Jesus said, "If you can believe, all things are possible to him who believes." (Mark 9:23, NKJV).

What would you do if your world suddenly turned dark and you wondered what to do about the dire circumstances of your life?

We often claim to have a strong faith, but we sometimes fall short when we're confronted with unfortunate circumstances. That's because all that we see in our three-dimensional realm influences our thinking and feelings. This often changes our thought patterns to negative ones and disrupts whatever tranquility our lives may have had before. In such situations, we must not simply accept reality as it is; instead, we need to trust in God who dwells in the fourth-dimensional realm. Through trust, you will be able to overcome the dire circumstances in which you find yourself.

By placing your trust in God, He will see your faith and grant you the grace to overcome the situation. He will also perform miracles in your behalf. No matter what circumstances you may be placed in, think of God and stand fast in your faith in Him. As you do so, you will experience God's working in your life.

The incident I'm about to share with you happened approximately twenty years ago. I was scheduled to lead a major revival meeting in Adelaide, Australia, followed by one in Perth; but due to an Australian Air strike, all flights were canceled. To get to Perth from Adelaide, it took a large aircraft three hours, and a small private plane five hours. So I called the meeting coordinator in Perth and explained to him that due to the strike I wouldn't be able to lead the revival meeting in Perth. But he explained to me that canceling could not be an option since so many people were already waiting at the meeting site; therefore, he said that they would send a private plane to get me.

When the airplane arrived, I noticed it was a manually operated one, and it didn't have a navigational system. So the pilot had to fly over the highways in order to get his bearings. We took off, but three hours or so later, we found ourselves headed into a big storm. The dark clouds drastically limited our visibility. The fact was that we were in complete darkness and couldn't see a thing!

When at last the pilot was no longer able to fly the plane, he turned to me for help as his last desperate measure. He said, "Hang onto the control lever. I'll have to utilize the radio frequency to reconfigure my flight coordinates."

As you can imagine, I was utterly dismayed by what I was hearing. But I also knew that desperate moments require desperate measures. Therefore I did whatever I could to help out. On the threshold of death, I had no choice but to rely on God. So I cried out to the Lord, as I hung tightly to the control lever: "Lord, save us!" Passing through that storm was an absolutely hellish experience.

We had to fly through that storm for nearly two hours. Finally we saw a faint light in the distance. It was the glow rising from the city of Perth. It was such a relief to us, for that light signified that we had moved from death to life and from darkness to light. We were able to land safely at the Perth airport by using the city's light as our guide. Everyone there thought our arriving safely was a miracle in itself. All credit was due to God. It was His grace and power that saved our lives. We weren't able to see with our own eyes, but God was leading us all the way, and we arrived at our destination safely.

Faith is being sure of what we hope for and certain of what we do not see. (See Heb. 11:1, NIV). In our relationship with God, faith is an absolute prerequisite. Hebrews 11:6 says, "But without faith it is impossible to please Him, for he who comes to God must believe that He is, and that He is a rewarder of those who diligently seek Him" (NKJV). If we don't have faith, we can't receive what God has in store for us. Faith is what connects the intention of your heart to God's will and actualizes it in your life.

Therefore we must always dwell in Jesus Christ our Lord in faith. The Bible clearly teaches us that "…in the gospel a righteousness from God is revealed, a righteousness that is by faith from first to last, just as it is written: 'The righteous will live by faith'" (Rom. 1:17, NIV). We must see God's world through the eyes of faith. The Bible says, "Now faith is being sure of what we hope for and certain of what we do not see"

(Heb. 11:1, NIV). Through the eyes of faith we are able to see what's not visible. If we look at God's grace in such a way, we'll actually see it manifest in our lives.

From now on, I hope you will become a seer of reality through the laws of faith and trust in our Lord in the midst of all negative circumstances and thoughts. Once you become a doer of the laws of faith, you will live a victorious life.

Plant the Seed and Anticipate the Harvest

God has directed me to seek first His kingdom, then to plant seed in faith. As I do so, I always anticipate miracles. When the construction for the Yoido church began, I offered to God the first house (in Nhengchun-dong, Seoul) that I had worked so hard to own. While I was praying, God spoke these words to me, *"Plant your house as a seed to Me. If you do, I will perform a miracle through it."*

I was around thirty years old at the time and was a married man. Therefore, having to offer my precious home to God was extremely difficult for me, even though I was a pastor. But I obeyed. Then God performed a great miracle. He allowed us to purchase the land in Yoido to build a church and to use the site to do great ministry for Him. It wasn't the amount I gave to God that was important, but my seed of obedience in faith that God looked upon so favorably.

Humans reap whatever they plant. Those who plant little will get little, but those who plant a lot will get a lot. This is not only a law of nature, but it is also a law of spirituality before God. It's important to remember, though, that we cannot reap without planting first. And if you plant, you must anticipate the day of harvest. Do you know of any farmer who only plants and does not anticipate the day of harvest? We must have faith that we can offer everything to God. It is only through faith that you can expect great miracles.

Galatians 6:7-9 says, "Do not be deceived, God is not mocked; for whatever a man sows, that he will also reap. For he who sows to his flesh will of the flesh reap corruption, but he who sows to the Spirit will of the Spirit reap everlasting life. And let us not grow weary while doing good, for in due season we shall reap if we do not lose heart" (NKJV). Plant and reap in God according to the laws of the Holy Spirit, and this will be the source of your blessings.

Improve the Content of Your Prayers

Once you feel full confidence that you have already received what you seek, and you have no doubt that it has been granted, and you've done everything you could possibly do in your prayers, and still nothing has taken place, then it's time to change the words of your prayers. Continuing to pray, "Heal me, O Lord, and grant me your mercy," without true faith in your heart will not avail much.

If you have already begun to seek for something, you need to pray along these lines: "Thank you, O Lord, for healing me. Thank you for already healing me. Now help me to be better." It sometimes takes time for symptoms to disappear, but this does not mean that healing has not already occurred. If the Holy Spirit has already given you the confirmation that you're healed, but you are still praying, "Heal me, O Lord, and fix me, Lord," you will cause God to question why you are doubting so much. Such an approach is unbelief, not faith.

Parents pray earnestly for their non-believing children, and at some point in time they feel conviction in their hearts that their prayer has been accepted. It is then they will know that all of their children will be saved some day. However, after a long time passes, and the children are still living lives of indifference toward God, some doubts might creep in. This happens because reality seems to indicate something different from what the parents had hoped for.

Let me encourage you to pray like this at such times: "O Father God! My first son has been saved, so call out to him. My daughter is saved as well, so help her to turn her life around. My last child, too, has been saved, so don't allow him to wander in the world anymore." This is a prayer of faith.

Praying for a new job works in a similar manner. If you have been praying earnestly for a good job, assurance will grow in your heart that you've already got a good job. However, if you continue to pray, "God, grant me a job," ignoring that assurance, then God won't be pleased with your prayers. In such circumstances, pray something like this: "God, thank you for giving me a great job! Since you've already granted it to me, make it visible so that I can see it. Help me to see it clearly, this new job you've given me."

When you start to believe in something you can't see, then it's time to speak as if that invisible thing is actually there before your eyes. Such prayers are rooted in the principles of faith, and when they are applied accordingly, you won't need to repeat the same thing over and over again. Instead, you can simply let God know what you're seeking, and you can do so with utter conviction.

Fight the Immediate Surroundings that are Tempting You in Negative Ways.

There are so many temptations that are aimed at getting you to give up your faith. Fight them off. Pray until you have peace in your heart. As you do so, cry out passionately to the Lord.

In God we are able to see, believe, and dream. When we pay attention to what we see with our eyes, however, we will become disappointed. All too often people give up when this happens. But we must never give up. We must fight off all negative temptations and influences in our lives. Those who are persistent and fight until the end will see that which they have been seeking in faith become fulfilled before their eyes.

"I Believe, but It's Too Hard to Believe."

Back in 1960, the year when our church experienced a phenomenal revival, we started an unprecedented all-night Friday prayer meeting. In those days, there were no such meetings or services in Korea. Nonetheless, we went ahead with this idea, and, as a result, all-night prayer meetings have now spread all over Korea.

Our first all-night prayer service lasted until 4:00 a.m., and we prayed and praised together, sharing our testimonies voluntarily. Our passion and desire to seek God through prayer and praise was greater than anything I had experienced before. It went so well that we felt that time passed too quickly. Many who came then were healed and blessed as they sought God.

Likewise, many experienced the infilling of the Holy Spirit and their desperate prayers were answered.

I recall one incident in particular. After I had finished praying for members who needed a physical healing, I made the following declaration: "Today our mighty God healed someone here who had an ulcer."

Then a young man stood up abruptly and said, "Pastor, that person is me. God just healed me! Wow, I really can't believe this, but … but … I don't know … hmm … I can't believe it … I just can't!"

I still vividly remember what that young man had cried out during the prayer meeting. His instinctual response, "I believe, Lord" turned into a declaration of doubt, "No. . . no, I can't believe." Before I go on any further, I might add here that this was an honest confession from him. Many people often say, "I believe," but then they turn around and begin to doubt. Belief is not something we create, nor is it a feeling we experience. No, belief is something that transcends our feelings and all of our immediate surroundings and circumstances.

That young man was a student at Yonsei University [a prestigious university in Korea] at the time. But he was suffering gravely from an ulcer, and he frequently vomited blood and even contemplated death. Because he bled so much, he really believed he would die before long. Therefore, he desperately sought God; he did everything he could to place his trust in God, only to be disappointed that deep down inside he really couldn't.

I cried out to God and asked Him to impart the faith that I had within me into the young man. I laid my hand on his head and prayed earnestly for him. I knew I had to do something to alter his fourth dimension first. I really wanted him to take on the thinking that he had already been healed through his unquestionable faith in God and that there was a bright future ahead of him.

God did work mightily in his life, as he later regained his health and became a man of faith. He eventually entered a seminary, finished his theological studies, became an ordained Presbyterian minister, and is now leading one of the most vibrant ministries in Korea.

No matter how desperately we try to cling to our faith, the world wastes no time in trying to pull us into despair and leading us to believe certain worldly notions that erode our faith by saying that such things as supernatural healings don't occur in this world. Even if we hold steadfast to the promises of God that are found in His Word and plant our feet firmly in faith, such pressures may still weigh down on us and cause us to yield to doubt. But we must overcome this tendency with the strength that God has already bestowed upon us. You can be an overcomer through Him.

Melt the Icy Wall of Disbelief with Prayers that Cry Out from Your Heart

The Scriptures clearly tell us to believe in the power of prayer and to trust that what we pray for will come about. However, there are times when no matter how much you pray, you just don't believe that what you're praying for is going to happen. We must keep on praying until we can actually believe we have received what we've been praying for.

There is a thick "ice wall" between belief and doubt in the human heart. We must melt it down. However, it won't melt by cold wind. Only the heat from fervent, passionate prayers can melt that wall down. When we come to the Lord with such prayers, then that wall will melt. The reason most people fall into despair and give up without achieving the needed assurance in their hearts is because they weren't able to melt the ice wall. Once that wall comes down, you can cling to the hand of assurance—the conviction within your heart.

Matthew 7:7-8 says, "Ask, and it will be given to you; seek, and you will find; knock, and it will be opened to you. For everyone who asks receives, and he who seeks finds, and to him who knocks it will be opened" (NKJV).

Jesus promised to give us answers that are bigger and wider than what we are able to conjure up in our minds. Therefore, we must pray until the ice wall melts and we have the assurance in our hearts. Once we do, we must verbally admit that we have already received it.

Isaiah 55:6-7 says, "Seek the LORD while He may be found, call upon Him while He is near. Let the wicked forsake his way, and the unrighteous man his thoughts; let him return to the Lord, and He will have mercy on him; and to our God, for He will abundantly pardon" (NKJV).

Charles Spurgeon, the renowned British pastor, said, "Lifting up prayers is like pulling on a big bell that resonates close to God's ears." This means that God will act swiftly once we pull on the "bell cord" of prayer. We must pray earnestly, persistently, and without ceasing. God will surely respond to our prayers.

Prayers rooted in faith turn our absolute despair into absolute hope. Some people are critical of those who pray out loud. But in Jeremiah 33:3 we read:"Call to Me, and I will answer you, and show you great and mighty things, which you do not know" (NKJV). Earnest prayers are prayers that cry out to God.

Psalm 145:19 says,"He will fulfill the desire of those who fear Him; He also will hear their cry and save them" (NKJV). We likewise must cry out to Him until we have assurance and peace in our heart. Prayers with a passionate pursuit will be answered.

Cast Your Three-Dimensional Realm onto God

We live in a very insecure world that is full of despair and uneasiness, but God wants you to let go of your worries and concerns. Therefore, cast your burden of negative thoughts and fears onto Him, and focus your eyes upon Him!

There is a very famous Korean poem by Songgang Chung Chul in *Hoonminga*. This poem describes a young man who sees an old man who is heavily sweating while he is carrying a heavy load. The young man has pity on the old man and wants to take the load from him so that he can travel more comfortably.

What Jesus said is pretty much the same thing. Jesus felt pity for people who were laden with heavy yokes. He still does. He said,"Come to me, all you who are weary and burdened, and I will give you rest" (Matt. 11:28, NIV). He extends an invitation to us to live a life with fewer burdens.

He asks, "*Is your yoke too heavy to bear? Is the load of the world too heavy for you? Is the yoke you carry the result of the devil's temptations? Are you laden with disease and illnesses? Are the pressures of your job too heavy? Is life too burdensome for you? Do you labor under the fear of death?*"

If your answer to these questions is "Yes," He issues this invitation to you: "*Cast your burdens upon Me. Let Me carry them for you. I've already taken those burdens upon myself as I hung on the cross, so just trust Me and obey Me. Then you shall lead a much easier life.*" What an amazing invitation our Lord has given to us!

The Lord Is My Shepherd

I always have the following words hidden in my heart, and I recite them whenever fear is looming on the horizon: "Depart from me, fear. God is my tower of refuge. 'I will say of the LORD, "He is my refuge and my fortress, my God, in whom I trust." Surely he will save you from the fowler's snare and from the deadly pestilence. He will cover you with his feathers, and under his wings you will find refuge; his faithfulness will be your shield and rampart. You will not fear the terror of night, nor the arrow that flies by day, nor the pestilence that stalks in the darkness, nor the plague that destroys at midday. A thousand may fall at your side, ten thousand at your right hand, but it will not come near you. You will only observe with your eyes and see the punishment of the wicked. If you make the Most High your dwelling—even the LORD, who is my refuge—then no harm will befall you, no disaster will come near your tent'" (Ps. 91:2-10, NIV).

Even if the sky were to come down and the land were to subside, God's promise will not change a speck. If we believe in His words and look to Him for guidance, while verbally confessing our faith, God's words shall work mightily in all our lives.

Our present society is treading near the gorge of insecurity. In Korea, for example, there is a great fear of war that has become a stronghold in many people's minds. This is especially true with regard to the tension caused by North Korea's testing of nuclear weapons and missiles. Likewise, the war in Iraq is causing fear and anxiety around the world. Many wonder if the same thing that has happened in Iraq will take place on the Korean peninsula. Some of us may be better at pretending to be calm than others, but the fear of war remains in the back of our minds.

Also, there's a widening gap between generations throughout the world. The different generations, for example, often have differing political views. The younger generation may unfairly conclude that all older people are conservatives. Members of the older generation, on the other hand, may try to push members of the younger generation to one side, seeing them as progressive reformists.

But the troubles don't stop there. An economic recession has made things more difficult overall. Some boast about growing exports while the domestic economy remains very gloomy. Credit defaults are on the rise and so are the costs of living and unemployment. These conditions serve to bring worries and anxiety to people. In addition, certain outbreaks of mysterious diseases from China and Southeast Asia are causing major concerns. Some of these diseases develop without detection, and there are few preventive measures that are effective against them.

In attempts to alleviate all this anxiety, certain retreats and meetings have been conducted. Likewise, many books have been written about various sicknesses and ways of dealing with anxiety and worry. Approximately one million books dealing with sickness, anxiety, and worries are printed annually. At the same time, palm readers and other occultists are experiencing a great rise in their clientele, and the number of patients receiving psychotherapy has increased significantly as well.

The twentieth century was a century of wars. Death tolls from war casualties and massacres during the preceding century number somewhere between 120,000,000 people and 180,000,000 people. From 1945 until the 1990's only three weeks have gone by without war taking place somewhere on planet Earth.

Presently our society is passing through the valley of fear and death. The world, therefore, is enshrouded in gloom. Most people don't realize this, but visiting a psychic reader or receiving psychiatric treatments is not helpful. Only Jesus Christ, our Shepherd, can rescue us from the valley of death. The God who possesses all authority over Heaven and earth offers His hands to us as we walk this gloomy path. Therefore, we must remain vigilant and cling to our Lord's hand as we plow through the valley of darkness. The Good Shepherd of the sheep will lead us and keep us safe with His rod and staff. (See Ps. 23). The Lord's staff is like a guiding hand. Jesus said, "To him the doorkeeper opens, and the sheep hear his voice; and he calls his own sheep by name and leads them out" (John 10:3, NKJV). The Lord is our Shepherd, and we are His sheep.

He knows our names, and He calls out our individual names, as He leads us with His staff.

Practice Living in Faith!

Practice living in faith and walking with God in your daily life. Meet the Holy Spirit, meditate on the Word and focus on God. Surround yourself with other men and women of faith.

No matter how much we try to claim how strong we are, we are feeble creatures. In fact, human beings are finite beings. We try constantly to renew ourselves by getting up on our own two feet, only to fall at our own peril. Even so, God has pity on us, because He knows we are helpless beings, and He desires to take care of us. We ought to be grateful for this. God gave us the Word so that we would be able to live victorious lives, and He sent the Holy Spirit to help us. Therefore, we must meditate on His Word without ceasing and cultivate a personal relationship with Him. We must go forth with other men and women of faith.

Growing Faith through the Word

Dwight L. Moody, who made a tremendous spiritual impact on America during the nineteenth century, made a vow to God that he would live a perfect life. This happened soon after he was born again. However, he was unable to keep his vow, because he found that his life was filled with stumbles and falls. Troubled by the contradictions within his life, he secluded himself upon a "prayer mountain" in order to pray. He also sought out all the revivals in town, but the blessings he received from these meetings only lasted a month or so.

Moody lamented about this by saying, "The seed of the Word can't grow in the field of my heart; it's like the seeds scattered on the street."

One day, he stumbled onto the following passage from the Book of Romans: "But they have not all obeyed the gospel. For Isaiah says, *'LORD, who has believed our report?'* So then faith comes by hearing, and hearing by the word of God" (Rom. 10:16-17, NKJV).

While reading this passage from Romans, Moody was awakened to a new spiritual understanding, and this awakening sparked something in his faith. The enlightenment involved his renewed faith in the Word, and he discovered that he was able to return to it whenever he felt his faith weakened. After discovering a way to restore faith from the Word, he meditated on the Word every morning and prayed to God for stronger faith. To help nurture his faith, he verbally confessed and claimed the Word and tried to practice it in all aspects of his life.

Moody went on to become one of the giants of faith who shook the world with the gospel's message. He wrote, "The Bible at times became a bed to lie on, a torch in times of darkness, a tool when I was working, a musical instrument when I praised God, a teacher when I was ignorant and a rock of foundation when I took false steps."

The Leap of Faith through the Holy Spirit

One important figure who made an impact on eighteenth-century England is John Wesley, the founder of Methodism. When Wesley was a student at Oxford University, he surrendered his life and passion to God. He then became a missionary and sailed across the ocean to America. However, he failed miserably as a missionary. Then a crisis of faith befell him, as he returned to England with deep disappointment in his heart. While sailing back home, a terrible storm that put everyone in grave danger threatened the sailing vessel. Everyone on board, including Wesley, began to run about in confusion. A group of Moravian believers overcame the fear that had been caused by the storm by praising God and trusting in Him. Witnessing all that happened during this crisis caused Wesley to be greatly astounded.

Soon thereafter, on May 24, 1738, Wesley experienced a powerful anointing of the Holy Spirit at Aldersgate in London. He described the experience as follows: "I went to the gathering at Aldersgate that evening because my friend had strongly pressed me to go. A person was reading the preface to Luther's translation of the Book of Romans. Around 9:15 p.m., he started explaining about the power of God that can stir a change within the hearts of people through faith in Jesus Christ. At that moment, I felt a blazing fire burning in my heart. I realized that through faith in Christ I'm claimed righteous and am forgiven of my sins, leading to my salvation in the truth of God's promise."

Wesley had read Romans 10:16-17 prior to that experience, but because he had read it with his head only, and not with his heart, it had been a mere intellectual exercise for him. During the evening at Aldersgate, however, he had truly experienced the power of the Word. It came in the form of a blaze in his heart, and he truly realized the meaning of forgiveness and righteousness through faith. A great light shone upon his spirit, and he experienced a truly great and pervading sense of joy deep within. He said that his heart had been "strangely warmed."

From then on, Wesley started sharing the gospel, which ultimately caused a great stir throughout England. Many asked Wesley how he mustered the strength to do what he had done. He answered them by saying, "I've always treasured the experience at Aldersgate deep down in my heart, and with that I was able to accomplish great things."

However, it's important to realize that we don't change simply because we know the truth. When our heart experiences the great truth from God through the Holy Spirit, it is that which gives us the courage and the strength to overcome any trials or tests. In communion with the Holy Spirit, Wesley grew in faith. We too should fill our hearts with the blaze of the Holy Spirit and walk with Him.

The Holy Spirit who sparked a fire in Wesley's heart desires to do the same thing within us. He helps us to know the truth and to remember the times when we've come to the light of truth. We need the Holy Spirit for our fourth-dimensional faith; it is He who will bring it to pass in our lives. Faith isn't something that is created by our effort, but it is the grace and gift of God for those who seek it.

Romans 8:26-27 says, "Likewise the Spirit also helps in our weaknesses. For we do not know what we should pray for as we ought, but the Spirit Himself makes intercession for us with groanings which cannot be uttered. Now He who searches the hearts knows what the mind of the Spirit is, because He makes intercession for the saints according to the will of God" (NKJV). The Holy Spirit intercedes for us every time we desperately need Him. He prays for us and guides us ceaselessly. It is only through the help of the Holy Spirit that we can understand and know God's will as it is revealed in the Word.

Union of Faith with Spiritual Companions

People of faith can greatly solidify their faith by uniting with other men and women of faith. Jesus reminds us, "Where two or three are gathered together in My name, I am there in the midst of them" (Matt. 18:20, NKJV).

It's important to know also that where there is even one righteous man, God will bless the very place where he stands. When we enter into fellowship with other men and women of faith, we expand the territory of the Kingdom of God. And from such unity we gain the strength we need to stand up against the world. Not only that, but we also become the very source of strength for others who look upon us for inspiration.

In 1969, a few weeks before Dwight Eisenhower, a former president of the United States, passed away at the Walter Reed Army Hospital, Billy Graham visited him and spoke with him for thirty minutes. When Billy Graham got up to walk out of his room, President Eisenhower grabbed him by the arm and said, "Pastor, could you stay a little longer? Please be with me."

"Yes, did you have something on your mind?"

"Pastor, I don't feel like I'm ready to meet the Lord. Could you help me?"

Billy Graham explained, "Only Jesus Christ can forgive us of our sins and accept us as His children. But we must believe that He suffered for our sins, died on the cross, and was resurrected from death. This has never been based on our merits."

He then grabbed Eisenhower's hands and prayed for him. In tears, Eisenhower thanked the evangelist:"Thank you, pastor. I think I'm ready to meet the Lord. There is so much peace in my heart right now."

President Eisenhower passed away not long after that visit, and he was in good spirits when he did. Billy Graham's conviction that was reflected in the prayer he prayed, gave President Eisenhower true peace as he placed his faith in God.

If you ever feel that your faith isn't strong enough, seek out another person to be your spiritual companion. There is much wisdom in asking him or her to intercede in your behalf. Prayers that are rooted in unified faith bring renewed conviction and peace.

Practicing Faith is for a Lifetime

As long as we live in this world, we need to be steadfast in our faith and plant our hopes in Heaven above. Even if our present circumstances seem dark and gloomy, we must look up to God and not focus on our immediate surroundings. We must hold onto our faith and keep trusting in God.

In the end God will work for our good because we love Him, and we have been called according to His purpose. (See Rom. 8:28.) This will happen as we strive to live in faith and develop spiritual habits in our lives. From the Word we must find ways to strengthen our faith and grow in faith. We must also seek communion with the Holy Spirit. We will strengthen our faith as we gather with other men and women of faith.

We shall experience marvelous things and miracles if we learn to live in faith. However, learning to live in faith does not happen overnight. In fact, it's a lifetime project. That's why it must become habitual in our lives. The people of faith we see in the Scriptures are people who have spent their lives learning and practicing their faith. This is how fourth-dimensional faith is nurtured and developed in our lives.

CHAPTER 4

Dreams

Change the Fourth-Dimensional Realm within You

The Bible says, "Where there is no revelation, the people cast off restraint; but happy is he who keeps the law" (Prov. 29:18, NKJV).

We must cherish our God-given dreams. People who attempt to live without revelation are doomed to perish. If there is no dream or vision within our heart today, there will be no tomorrow. If eggs aren't incubated, there won't be chicks. Therefore, we must live with dreams and visions in our hearts. In due time, our dreams and visions will hatch from their shells and manifest in our reality.

What do you dream? Do your dreams come from selfishness? We need to learn to be very discriminating about this. That's because greed that is conceived in the fourth-dimensional realm will be actualized in our three-dimensional lives. There is a huge difference between good dreams and greed. In good dreams there are hopes for tomorrow, but dreams that stem from greed lead us to break laws and commit crimes.

There is a reason why young Moses failed miserably in his attempts to rescue his people. Part of the problem was that he had envisioned the rescue based on his youthful vigor and his own plans. No matter what the dream is, if God isn't in it, selfish greed and ambitions will always destroy it. Abraham and Joseph, on the other hand, experienced victory in spite of hardships and afflictions. That's because they both dreamed with God.

When we dwell in God, there are certain dreams that He will give to us. He instills dreams within us through the Scriptures and the Holy Spirit, sometimes even while we listen to sermons and messages, and sometimes while we are praying. Dreams from God are much more grand and vast than any other kinds of dreams human beings may experience.

Moses dreamed of freeing his people, but God was dreaming of turning His people into a holy nation, a kingdom of priests. God spoke to Moses, "'And you shall be to Me a kingdom of priests and a holy nation.' These are the words which you shall speak to the children of Israel" (Exod. 19:6, NKJV). As such, God's dreams are bigger and wider than any other kinds of dreams. That's why we need to dream the boundless dreams of God. And like Joseph, we need to take hold of the dreams God gives to us. Through His dreams we are able to overcome the afflictions and difficulties of life.

The dreams we come to cherish through God are found in the fourth-dimensional realm. And those dreams manifest in our reality after we seize the third-dimensional realm. Now, examine your fourth-dimensional dreams and change them accordingly. The following points will show you how to change your dreams.

Always wait on God to give you glorious and amazing dreams. Don't ever allow yourself to dream of your path becoming a dead-end. Hope and wait on God in full anticipation that He will give you awesome dreams.

Like someone standing on the edge of a steep cliff, there are moments in our lives when problems become too difficult for us to resolve on our own. At such times the Scripture reminds us, "Nothing is impossible with God." That's absolutely right!

When we think despair lies ahead of us, God says there is hope. God carries out mysterious works that we will never be able to fully comprehend. All we have to do at such times is to place our trust in our God, the One who moves in mysterious ways. What's even more amazing is that when we trust Him and cherish those awesome dreams, God bestows miracles upon us. It is this knowledge that enables us to carry on with our lives.

In 1965, after attending a major assembly that was held in Brazil, I went back to the Rio de Janeiro Airport to wait for my plane. A man who looked like a local policeman approached me and asked to see my passport. Without any hesitation, I handed it to him. You won't believe what he did next. This "officer" ran away with my passport! At that time, I didn't know anybody in Brazil, so I felt completely helpless. The time came to board the airplane, but I couldn't get on the plane. I didn't have any money with me, because I had only brought enough for the needs of the trip. My legs felt weak and I collapsed to the floor. I had no choice but to cry out to God.

I prayed, "God, have pity on me! What am I going to do? God, did you not say all things work together for the greater glory of God? Well, I love you dearly, and following your will, I came all this way to Brazil to be your witness and share the gospel here in Rio de Janeiro. Only you and you alone can help me now. Lord, I believe that all things do work for your glory. Reach out to me!"

I continued to pray and to seek His guidance. Some minutes passed and then a man wearing a suit approached me.

"Excuse me, aren't you Pastor Yonggi Cho?" I turned around to make sure there was no one else behind me that the man could be speaking to.

Then I said, "Yes, I am. I'm Yonggi Cho. How do you know my name?"

"I have a missionary friend, Louis P. Richards, who went out to Korea on a mission about ten years ago. He once sent me a written testimony with your picture on it. I remember being deeply moved by reading your testimony. But it's so amazing to see you here in front of me. And also, it's hard to believe that I can remember a face from a picture I saw ten years ago. But what brings you to Brazil? I had to see someone off—a friend from Sao Paulo—today. I was about to leave when I saw you; I thought I would come over and see if it really is you."

I thought I would burst into tears at that moment. How great and big is the grace of God. I was stunned. My Lord had immediately responded to my prayer. After I composed myself, I began to tell him the whole story. He then told me that this kind of thing happened often in Brazil, especially to foreign visitors from third-world countries.

He said, "You were so naïve, pastor. Those kinds of people usually ask for money. If you give them some change, they won't take your passport. Anyway, I'm glad nothing worse happened."

With the gentleman's help, I returned safely to Korea. I still thank God to this day over that incident. I wonder what would have happened if God hadn't heard my prayers. God is so good. He is so great. He is able to pull us out of all of life's quagmires. Through this incident my faith in God was strengthened and I felt His love deep down within.

You, too, can experience this amazing love from God. I don't believe God favored me because I am His servant or because I'm special in any way. God shall reveal great things to you, too, as long as you hold steadfast to your faith, look up to Him and surrender your will to Him. I sincerely hope you will get to experience His amazing work in your lives.

The exodus of the Israelites from Egypt illustrates how great and awesome God's plan was toward His people. Through Moses, God freed the Israelites from the 430 years of bondage and slavery they had endured. But there were still obstacles to face.

For example, they had to get across the Red Sea in order to get to Canaan. Hundreds of Egyptian chariots were following close on their heels. This, of course, meant that there could be no turning back. The people began to murmur and complain. They resented the fact that Moses had brought them out of

Egypt, and they felt that their doom was now assured. The Red Sea was in front of them, and the Egyptian armies were behind them!

Right then, however, God appeared to Moses, and He instructed him to look to Him. He assured him that He would take care of the situation, and directed Moses to hold out his hand. He said, "The Lord will fight for you, and you shall hold your peace" (Exod. 14:14, NKJV). When Moses stretched out his hand over the sea, the waters parted, enabling the Israelites to cross over. (See Exod. 14:21). The Egyptians all drowned when they tried to follow the Israelites.

God never forsook them. How could anyone have known this before it happened, however? The Egyptians certainly didn't know, and the Israelites were full of doubt; but Moses believed God, followed His instructions, and everything changed. God had something in store for His people that no human being could possibly imagine.

When Moses held out his staff, the Red Sea split in half. The Israelites, witnessing this, repented and clung firmly to the powerful hand of their God. And everyone crossed through the sea safely. The Egyptian chariots continued their chase into the Red Sea, but the waters swallowed them alive.

This wasn't some natural occurrence that happened by mere chance. Rather, God displayed His awesome, mysterious plan and His might through this event so that all would be able to witness it. This same God is ready and willing to display His power in our lives as well.

The Bible says, "But as it is written: '*Eye has not seen, nor ear heard, nor have entered into the heart of man the things which God has prepared for those who love Him*'" (1 Cor. 2:9,

NKJV). Firmly believe in God's awesome blessings and in His love. As you do so, you will soon discover that He has many wonderful things in store for you.

God created the universe, and He created humans on the last day. He first created the habitat in which humans were to live—the world He wanted us to subdue and have dominion over. God provided all that we as humans needed, and because He loved us so much, He allowed us to rule over what He created. In the same way that God planned a whole new creation for Adam and Eve, He has plans for each one of us to be born again through faith in Christ.

Throughout all eternity our Lord had our salvation in mind. We did not somehow accidentally commit sin and then by coincidence become the beneficiary of forgiveness and salvation. Before the foundation of the world the cross of Jesus Christ had already been prepared to rescue us from our sins.

Genesis 3:15 says, "And I will put enmity between you and the woman, and between your seed and her Seed; He shall bruise your head, and you shall bruise His heel" (NKJV). This passage gives a hint about what would eventually happen. We must acknowledge and believe that the work of Christ on the cross wasn't a mere afterthought in God's mind, but it was an event that He had thoroughly planned in advance. Our Lord came into this world in human form. He was born into the world through the Virgin Mary. In the birth of Jesus we learn what the above verse means. Jesus, who was born of the Virgin Mary, was sent from God to conquer Satan. God had this plan in mind long before the fall of Adam and Eve.

Six hundred years before the birth of Christ, the prophet Isaiah predicted the suffering of Christ on the cross: "Surely He has borne our grief and carried our sorrows; yet we esteemed Him stricken, smitten by God, and afflicted. But He was wounded for our transgressions, He was bruised for our iniquities; the chastisement for our peace was upon Him, and by His stripes we are healed" (Isa. 53:4-5, NKJV).

This passage alludes to the fact that God had developed the plan of salvation through Jesus Christ long before the Fall. The reason we are saved by believing in Jesus Christ is found in the fact that God had prepared the road to salvation well in advance.

As a result, you have become someone who understands a great and tremendous secret: You are forgiven of your sins by believing in Christ. This is how vast God's love and power are. No one can understand this great truth through mere knowledge or intuition. God transcends all human knowledge. Therefore we must believe in our hearts what He has done for us and provided for us. No matter what we face in our lives, we must not ever allow ourselves to become perturbed. We must believe that God is in control. We may not have a plan, but God does.

Keep these prophetic words in your heart: "Thus says the LORD who made it, the LORD who formed it to establish it (the LORD *is* His name): 'Call to Me, and I will answer you, and show you great and mighty things, which you do not know'" (Jer. 33:2-3, NKJV).

Have faith in God's promises and believe them firmly. We are truly blessed people, and we are part of God's awesome and mysterious plan.

We must always dream as if awesome and mysterious events are going to occur in our lives. Do not ever allow yourself to dream of darkness pervading your life. Instead, dream positive and optimistic dreams, dreams that are full of high hopes, and do so in good faith regarding God's good promises. Believe that God will surely manifest His wonderful works in your life, and as you anticipate His miracles, keep your heart and your mouth open. He will fill your heart and your mouth, and He is completely able to provide all that you need and much more.

Once there was a mother who had been divorced, and she lived with her small son in the poorest of circumstances. They went about their lives on a day-to-day basis, but they were barely able to make ends meet.

The young boy frequently fretted and cried. One day he said, "Mom, buy me a cat. Please. I'd like to have a cat."

Unfortunately, the mother had no money to buy her son a cat. This caused her to be disappointed and she began to grieve over the circumstances of her life.

Her son pled with her, "My friend has a dog and a cat. Why won't you get me a pet?"

After the mother calmed him down, she told him, "Son, why don't we pray to our good heavenly Father. God will surely give us a cat for a present."

Then they both began to pray with their hands firmly clasped together.

She prayed, "Father, you know our dire circumstances. Please give us a cat. We have no money to buy a cat. Father

God, we earnestly pray to you. Have mercy on us. We pray in Jesus' name."

The son asked his mother, "Do you really believe God will send us a cat?"

"Absolutely! Our God is able. A cat! That's nothing for Him, son. I'm sure He will ... let's just wait and see. If He doesn't, we'll just continue to pray. He listens to all our prayers. Let's just keep praying and dream that He will bring this to pass."

The two of them continued to pray for several days.

Then, on a hot, sunny summer day, as the mother was knitting in their front yard and the son was scribbling on a piece of paper next to her, something amazing happened. They both saw something dark falling out of the sky, and they were completely shocked by what they saw. A cat falling out of the sky? They just couldn't believe it. They both jumped up and down in total happiness and joy. God had answered their prayer. This story spread like wildfire all over America. It even found its way into the newspapers under this headline: "A Cat Out of the Sky."

As time passed, a man appeared at their doorstep. He claimed to be the owner of the cat and told the mother and her son that he wanted to take the cat home with him. It all seemed so absurd. The man explained that he lived 800 km away from them. He told them that one day the cat climbed a tree and didn't come down from it, and he had desperately tried to get it down without success. Finally, he tried to bend the tree limbs, but he accidentally let go of the limbs, and the cat sprang out of the branches into the sky and disappeared!

The man believed that his cat had flown 800 km and landed in their front yard.

After explaining all this, he demanded that they give the cat back to him. But the mother and her son didn't believe his story. They told him that the cat was a gift from God. Ultimately, the matter went to court. The court then ordered some men to conduct an experiment. They tried to simulate what the man claimed had happened. They repeated the experiment numerous times to confirm their finding and discovered that something with the cat's weight would not fly more than twenty to thirty meters. The experiments did not provide proof of what the man was claiming. In the end, therefore, the court ruled in favor of the mother and the child, and they called the cat "the gift from God."

This story goes beyond the scope of most of our day-to-day experiences. Even so, it helps us to see that God is someone able to perform spectacular and miraculous things for His people. Therefore, you are able to dream something as seemingly absurd as this story. Remember, if you dream big, your big dreams will lead you through the difficult times of life. So dream and anticipate God's amazing works. Then these things will become yours. You must believe that God has many wonderful things in store for you. Dream that He's going to perform these things in your life. Don't let go of your hope, and keep on praying that your dreams will become reality. I can assure you that your dreams will truly become yours someday.

First, register your dreams in your heart. Then record the dreams with all their details in written form. Keep it in front of you, and pray until you have absolute certainty within your heart that you will achieve those dreams. As you do all this, be sure to examine your dreams in the light of the Word.

What do you dream? Create a written record of your dreams right now and place it somewhere that is easily accessible so you can refer to it often. I encourage you to do this because you need to remember your dreams and see them manifesting before your eyes. There is profound importance in this, because it enables you to see God at work in your life.

I once led a seminar on church growth for pastors in Australia. Their first reaction to my teaching was that church growth would be impossible in Australia. Many of them felt that such growth would be possible only in places like the US and Korea. They were quite pessimistic indeed. They also reasoned that most Australians were more into enjoying exercise and their leisure time instead of spiritual matters. The number of Australians who were attending church at that time was quite low.

In view of all this, on the last day of the seminar I proposed this to the group: "Get a piece of paper and a pencil. Write down what you've been praying for and what you hope the status of your church will be in two years. Also write down in detail just how many members you expect to have in your congregation in two years."

Everyone began to write down their expectations, visions, and dreams. They had different goals in mind. Some wrote down, "Fifty members in two years," while others wrote, "A Church of 100 members." Then there were others who wrote, "300 to 500 members."

I then went on: "Place that paper in a visible spot in your office. Look at it and pray over it day and night. Record the vision in your heart, and expect the Holy Spirit to work powerfully."

After two years had passed, I returned to Australia for another conference. The president of the Assemblies of God met me and, with tears in his eyes, he remarked,

"Pastor, our church had seen no growth in ten years. But as I dreamt and prayed, as you told us to do, we witnessed 100 percent growth in just two years! And it isn't just our church. Many other churches throughout Australia are experiencing growth as well."

This is a living proof of the power of dreaming and praying. Applying the principle of prayerful dreaming, one church in Australia grew to a congregation of thousands!

As I write this, I am dreaming of planting some 500 churches in various places throughout Korea. With clear goals and a detailed plan, I dream about this day and night. I also dream of holding all sorts of major assemblies throughout the world. The ultimate goal of my dream is to take the gospel to the uttermost parts of the world. So I wake up while dreaming that glorious vision and take that dream to sleep with me. When dreams are kept in their proper perspective, they will produce faith, and the Holy Spirit will work through them mightily and powerfully. That's why you must cherish your God-given dreams within your heart. Those dreams will become the very mighty hands of God that will mold and create your future.

During a trip to South America, I met a pastor by the name of Cabrera. Pastor Cabrera shared his own testimony about God's marvelous works with me. He told me how long ago, a mother brought to him a child without one ear and asked him to pray and lay his hands on the boy. While he was praying, Pastor Cabrera dreamed of God creating a brand-new ear for the boy. He prayed earnestly for this to happen. After some time had passed, much to his surprise, he saw what appeared to be a lump growing out of the side of the boy's head where there was no ear. He was quite shocked to witness this, but kept praying for the boy.

A while later, the boy and his mother returned for more prayer. So in faith the pastor prayed, and he dreamt once again of the boy receiving a new ear. He then told the child's mother to think as if her child had both ears and to recite every morning, "My precious baby, your ears are so pretty."

She did this, but nothing particularly different occurred. Nonetheless, the pastor carried on with the prayer, and he continued to dream. The next time when the mother brought her son for prayer, the pastor put his hand on the boy's head, prayed a prayer of faith, and when he opened his eyes, the lump that had started forming actually spread out like the opening of a folding fan! The boy had a new ear!

What an amazing work took place before their eyes. Only God could perform such a miracle. This is how dreams are fulfilled. Create and picture what you expect to have happen in faith. Eventually this will lead to a time when you will actually see everything you have imagined becoming manifest before your eyes.

Therefore, be sure your fourth-dimensional dreams are specific and detailed. This will ensure that what will appear in the three-dimensional realm won't be some obscure occurrence, but something that is real and specific when it is manifested. That is why you need to imagine what you want and use that as the focal point for the realization of your goals.

In order to achieve your dreams and to see them appear in all their elaborate detail, you will need to back them up with earnest prayer. One reason for fasting is to bring clarity to your fourth-dimensional realm. Fasting helps to remove any cloudiness that may be there. When we fast, we are cutting off the source that fuels our strong wills and makes us believe that "I can do this." Fasting leads us to let go of our own wills. In the process, we learn to look up to God and allow Him to change us. When we experience the changes He brings about, our fourth-dimensional realm will change as well. God works in our midst and helps us to see our dreams come to their fulfillment in all their minute details. Therefore I urge you to find clearer goals and dreams through prayer.

All athletes, heads of households, and sick patients share one thing in common: Each group has earnest desires or goals in mind. But we must be different from them. We must become individuals who dream the same dreams, but we must do so differently. We must look to the cross of Jesus Christ and dream of our spirits and bodies becoming free from any and all illnesses and wholeheartedly accept these goals with all their details in our hearts.

No matter what our present circumstances are or what the conditions of our lives may be, we must not be too ardently attached to and worried about them. We must open our hearts to receive the dreams of Christ. Peter writes, "Who Himself bore our sins in His own body on the tree, that we, having died to sins, might live for righteousness—by whose stripes you were healed" (1 Pet. 2:24, NKJV). We must accept Jesus' dreams through the cross. Then we shall experience a healing, and we will witness God's mighty power and have all of the stumbling blocks removed from our lives.

When we look to the cross, we must remember the blessings and goodness that were bestowed upon Abraham and the goals of his dream. We must first get rid of any stumbling blocks that may lead us to believe that our lives have been cursed with poverty. Then we must open our hearts to accept the kinds of blessings and goodness Abraham experienced. This, I believe, is the dream of Jesus for each one of us.

Galatians 3:13 says, "Christ has redeemed us from the curse of the law, having become a curse for us (for it is written, 'Cursed is everyone who hangs on a tree')" (NKJV). The kinds of goals and dreams we set must be the kinds that are "approved" by the cross of Jesus Christ.

Furthermore, it's very important for you to realize that the notion of eventual success in this world isn't applicable to us as believers, because the world isn't our *home*. There are special goals that may influence even the eternal world. Paul writes, "For we know that if our earthly house, this tent, is destroyed, we have a building from God, a house not made with hands, eternal in the heavens" (2 Cor. 5:1, NKJV). Let's look to Jesus who bore the cross on our behalf. And let's dream dreams. As we do so, our hopes will transcend the boundaries of the uttermost ends of the earth and reach into the heavens.

As incubators allow premature newborns to recuperate gradually, start from your "smaller" dreams and begin to cultivate them. Walk with the Holy Spirit as you commit yourself to even small, insignificant matters. As you do so, rise above all hardships.

Dreams that come from the cross must be planted before any fruit can be harvested. No matter how difficult your present circumstances might be, if you plant sanctified dreams with the help of the Holy Spirit, then your dreams will pervade the three-dimensional realm and start to cause changes within your life. You will be transformed from death to life, from chaos to order, from darkness to light, and from poverty to wealth. The changing point in your life will be realized through your fourth-dimensional dreams. So plant your dreams and be sure to cultivate them.

All human beings earnestly desire for changes to take place in their lives, and they want to accomplish their dreams. However, most people only wish to have their dreams fulfilled; they don't do any planning in advance, which is the most crucial element in accomplishing your dreams. If you have dreams, then you need to be sure that they will come true and start to believe as if you've already achieved them. This is advance planning. For unprepared individuals, dreams will remain just as dreams. To actualize one's dreams is often too difficult for many people.

The current sanctuary at Yoido Full Gospel Church has been expanded from the old one. As the church grew, I made plans to build a town that would surround the church, which would be in the middle of the town. We expanded the infrastructure by building a center that was dedicated to educational purposes, two missions headquarters, and other facilities. We also established a newspaper and named it *Kok-*

min Ilbo. We went on to make plans to build centers on Prayer Mountain as well.

We did all this because we saw the need for more facilities that would enable people to come and worship God in spirit and to have fellowship with other believers. When we started building the Yoido church, I had only $2,000 in my possession, but the necessary budget for the building project was set at around $2,000,000! In the face of this, I went to God and asked Him to help us to appropriate the necessary funds. I determined that God would be my source.

Once you firmly grab hold of the vision God gives and keep it in your heart with passion, you will discover that the issues of financing and budgeting will come last. God will take care of everything else.

We need to establish priorities as we endeavor to glorify God. First, we need to be sure that what we're dreaming and doing is the will of God. Second, we must establish clear-cut goals. Third, we need heart-felt passion to achieve those goals. Lastly, we must go forth in the faith that God will surely be with us until the end. Once all these matters are set in place, it's time to pull out a calculator and start paying the bills. In my case, I daringly pushed forward, believing that the needed money would be provided. In developing your plans, remember that the immediate surroundings and circumstances are insignificant. Simply stride forward in faith. It is God who will cause things to happen.

Expectant parents prepare for the arrival of their child by getting clothes, shoes, and a bed for the newborn. This is quite appropriate. Likewise, our dreams need certain basic preparations in order for them to be fulfilled. If a dream is born, there needs to be a *realistic* plan for it. We must rely on the Holy Spirit. That is the only way for dreams to be born and accomplished. Once the dream has been achieved, there also needs to be a place—a "dream bed"—in which you can lay the dream down.

I would like you to be prepared. God dreams that all His churches will share the gospel to the uttermost parts of the earth. We must strive toward achieving His dream, while realizing that God is our primary source. And as we move forward with God by our side, we will never be disappointed!

In Genesis 17 we read that God promised a child to Abram when he turned ninety-nine years of age. Abram and Sarai had no children, but God told them to desire a child as if they already had one. Then Abram became ninety-nine years old and Sarah was eighty-nine years old. They were both snowy-haired elders without any heirs. God made them change their names to Abraham, "the father of many generations" and Sarah, "the mother of many generations."

They must have wondered why God gave them such names, because they still didn't have any children. However, in God's mind, a child was on the way. The reason God told them to desire and claim the very thing they didn't have as if they did have it is because in God's mind everything is in the present tense. That means that Isaac was already born before God, but humans couldn't see him. That is why God told them to desire a son as if they already had one.

Believers must take on the faith that enables them to be convinced to the point that they are able to verbally admit that they have the very thing they don't seem to have. Our Lord tells us, "Therefore I say to you, whatever things you ask when you pray, believe that you receive them, and you will have them" (Mark 11:24, NKJV). Jesus charges us to think, see, and believe the very thing that isn't visible. Even if it may seem like you haven't received it, believe as if you already have received it.

In another passage, our Lord says, "For assuredly, I say to you, whoever says to this mountain, 'Be removed and be cast into the sea,' and does not doubt in his heart, but believes that those things he says will be done, he will have whatever he says" (Mark 11:23, NKJV). Here Jesus is explaining that before you tell the mountain to be removed and be cast into the sea, you must pray, believe, and accept (in your heart) that it has already been accomplished.

You must give all your heart and soul to whatever you are praying for. Someone might ask, "How long should one pray?" The answer is: until the Holy Spirit comes to your heart and speaks these words to you: "*Your prayer has been answered. It's been done.*" So pray until you are absolutely filled with the full conviction that the Holy Spirit will bring to your heart.

Whenever I begin to pray about something, the object usually seems quite distant in the beginning. But as I pray, "God, answer my prayer," then that which seems far off begins to draw closer to me. And one day, as I continue to pray, my heart will be filled with the full conviction that my prayer has been answered. Right then, I will start to see the very thing that isn't there yet, and I will begin to claim, "My prayer has been answered."

Many sick people will go up to Prayer Mountain to pray and fast over their illnesses. Now, as these people are ascending the mountain, full healing may seem very far away to them, almost beyond their reach. But as days pass by, and the sick person becomes fully engaged in fasting and prayer, he or she will feel a healing in his or her heart, and then a sense of full conviction will come to him or her and he or she will be able to say, "Yes, I'm healed!" Then the person will take notice of his or her body and think he or she isn't healed after all. These folk need to remember that when Jesus cursed the fig tree, it didn't shrivel immediately; instead, it died the next day. Likewise, even when one feels that he or she is fully healed, but finds that the illness is still with him or her, the individual needs to wait a few days after returning home in faith, and then he or she shall experience full recovery. Hallelujah!

It often takes time for something that is believed to become manifest. The principle that is at work regarding this is similar to what happens to uprooted grass, which doesn't die right away, but does so eventually. There is frequently a time of waiting for something that is believed to actually come to full fruition.

There was a member of our church who couldn't even walk a few steps due to a failing heart. Her doctor told her that surgery to open up her clogged arteries was mandatory. Even so, she postponed the surgery and instead went up Prayer Mountain and began to pray.

She prayed, "Father God, I offer you the money that would pay for the surgery. I would like to ask you to operate on me."

To unbelievers, nothing could be more foolish than this prayer. How can one who is suffering from clogged arteries get well without the necessary surgery? But this lady felt a conviction in her heart, and she heard a voice that said, "*Get up and move around!*"

What she had heard was the voice of our Lord. In her condition, she might have died if she did what the voice directed her to do. Nonetheless, her conviction was overwhelmingly strong, so she decided to get up and do as she was told. In the process, she didn't feel any shortness of breath, and she continued to pray.

Then she heard a voice telling her to run up to Elijah Peak and return. Elijah Peak is located halfway up the hill of our Prayer Mountain. Even for young healthy men, such a run would be difficult. But she did as she felt she was told to do, and she ran up to Elijah Peak! Like a normal, healthy person, she easily made the run up the hill. A miracle had occurred in her body. She believed in the unthinkable, and she was completely healed.

When coming before God with our prayers, we must pray until we are absolutely convicted that we have received His promise. Even if what we're praying for is overwhelmingly unthinkable, we must still pray for it. Such things as a non-believing spouse, what you dream for your children to become, dreams for your business, and a desire to be healed of some illness may seem like a veritable Mount Everest of problems. However, these things that are beyond your power will lead you to cry out to God. Therefore, cry out to Him and pray until you are fully convinced that God has heard and will answer your prayers.

The successor to the famous American steel giant, Andrew Carnegie of Carnegie Steel, was Charles Schwab. With only an elementary education, he began his career with the company as a worker who did odd jobs. Even though he was doing odd jobs, he worked hard and always kept his hopes up. He always gave his best, even to mundane and petty tasks. He always looked to the future and dreamed of becoming someone successful. In fact, he began to see himself as the owner of the company, and he handled everything from that point of view.

Every day he would clean every nook and cranny of the company. He cleaned these spaces as if they were his own room. Others mocked at his enthusiasm and diligence. But Charles ignored them and, rain or shine, he did his best to keep the company clean. All the while he kept on dreaming that one day he would become the owner of the company. Before long, everyone saw his genuine heart, and they began to give him moral support. Gradually Schwab was promoted to full-time work with the company.

Even after the promotion, he never lost his strong work ethic. He kept his owner-like attitude and continued to work diligently. It wasn't long before he became the "talk of the town."

President Carnegie was deeply touched by what he heard about Charles, and he recruited him to become his personal secretary. Charles was loyal to the president. He constantly reminded himself of his personal motto, "I shall work like the owner of this company and take on the right attitude. If I'm told to go five miles, I shall go ten; if someone asks for my shirt, I shall give him my jacket as well."

Deeply moved by Charles's dedication to the company, President Carnegie offered Charles $100,000 in bonus money at a time when the young man was making only two to three thousand dollars a year. President Carnegie complimented him at a company meeting and said that that no one can put a price value on someone who works with an owner-like attitude.

As President Carnegie's retirement grew near, everyone wondered who would be his successor. People began to talk about their personal favorites: a Harvard graduate, a Princeton graduate, or the heir of a rich, distinguished family.

To everyone's surprise, President Carnegie nominated Charles Schwab for the position, a man who had climbed up the ladder from odd jobs to becoming a personal secretary. Actually, the news shocked the whole world. President Carnegie stressed that the successor would be someone not of an educated or intelligent background, but someone who has on an owner-like attitude in all he does and dreams for the company. In short, President Carnegie thought such a person would be his best successor.

Give and do your best, no matter where you may be. God will help you. No matter how small and insignificant a task might seem to be, give it 100 percent! God is watching you, and He knows what's in your heart. He will certainly make use of your intentions and bless you with His benefits. I charge you to do your best and to keep your focus on God.

Dreams and wishes don't just happen to come true. To achieve them, everyone must travel through the tunnel of hardship. Dreams have a dear price. For them to be realized, our strong wills must be broken and we must come into obedience to the Lord through hardship and suffering. God always makes those who are treading the wrong path, the path of destruction—those who are living by their own wills, thoughts, and plans—to return to Him through trials. God has prepared so many things for every individual, and He will bless those who tread the path that has been prepared for them.

Dreams aren't cheap; everyone must pay a price to see them fulfilled. Suffering is God's plan for us because He knows it will break our stubborn wills and lead us to return to God in obedience. Suffering allows our faith to grow, and it actually strengthens it. Those who overcome suffering and trials are the ones who ultimately achieve their dreams.

People who work out physically do so to strengthen their bodies. The same principle applies to the spiritual realm. Our dreams and hopes are strengthened through trials. Suffering is the seed that grows into big dreams and hopes. Through suffering, we will be able to cross to the other side.

Suffering is like a tunnel through which we must pass in order to achieve our dreams. Without passing through that tunnel, one can only remain where he or she is presently. But as a result of passing through it, he or she shall be able to cross over to the other side. As we pass through the tunnel of hardships and trials, we enter the world of big dreams and hopes.

Peter writes, "That the genuineness of your faith, being much more precious than gold that perishes, though it is tested by fire, may be found to praise, honor, and glory at the revelation of Jesus Christ" (1 Pet. 1:7, NKJV). Afflictions are like a meal that is prepared on a table of dreams. That's because all dreams have their price, and to achieve them, the price must be paid. If one holds onto one's dreams, then he or she must eat from the table of afflictions. Eating from this table, figuratively speaking, causes him or her to gain more strength and courage and to move towards his or her dreams. To someone with dreams, hardships and trials may well seem insignificant. That's because they realize that such negative circumstances are nothing but a small step that needs to be taken on the road to seeing their dreams fulfilled.

You mustn't ever be disappointed because what you're seeking isn't yet visible. Have patience. Meditate on the suffering Jesus experienced on the cross. Live a life that is filled with hope and share your hope with others.

Do you believe that God is with you always? Do you trust that He will always protect you? This is what I mean by having hope in Him. We have a God who is always willing to help us. That's why we can do all things in Him. Anything that is thought, believed, and dreamed in God will come true. Therefore, I urge you to pray hard and earnestly, as you dream in the hope God gives to you, and never forget that you are God's chosen being.

I planted my first church after I graduated from seminary in 1958. It was a tent church that we set up in Bulkwang-dong, Daejo Village, a poverty-stricken area of Seoul. The Korean War had ended and the village was swarming with poverty, diseases, and disorder.

Seoul was teeming with war refugees, and people flocked there from all over Korea. They experienced dire conditions there, and Daejo-dong was worse than the rest of Seoul. The people there were destitute. It was then that I started sharing the message of the Gospel of Jesus Christ. It was certainly a ripe time for the light of God and the message of hope to reach the people who lived there.

I preached, "People, repent and receive Jesus Christ. Each and every one of you is precious before our God. Believe in Jesus Christ and you shall be saved!"

No one offered a retort to my crying out. Daejo-dong was full of alcoholics, thugs, and diseased people, but a particular incident occurred that sent tremors through this village and certainly paved the way for my ministry to be catapulted into full swing.

In the maze of the crowded shacks of that area, one particular shack stood out. It was so decrepit that it really was on the verge of collapsing. I decided to go there to pay a visit to its occupants, but it took a great deal of courage for me to do so. I stood in front of the hovel and asked, "Anybody home?"

A woman stuck her head out from the open door. "Who's there?" she cried. Her name was Cho-hee Lee, and she was a refugee from the Bookchung area, which was north of Seoul.

Cho-hee was a pitiful woman who had nine boys to take care of and a husband who was a drunkard. She suffered from a heart condition and ulcers, and her body was emaciated and bony. It's really hard for me to describe how she looked, for she was so thin and frail.

Right then and there, I decided to witness to her. From then on I visited her every day, and during each visit I witnessed to her about Jesus and Heaven. Every time I did so, she would say that all religious people are liars and she would argue with me angrily, saying that there couldn't be a Heaven in this messy world!

She said, "I'm not concerned about where I go after death. Death is insignificant; my life right now is literally hell. Look around you. You see how we live, don't you? I want to live well *now*, not after I die! You should just leave!"

She was "witnessing" to me instead of me witnessing to her! Everything she had said was absolutely true, from her point of view, at least. I listened to her and returned to the tent church. I couldn't forget what she had said to me, though. I realized that some of her words were true. She had said that Heaven must come into our lives right now, and I thought about this for a long time. Then it hit me. I thought, "That's it! Heaven is needed right now, not later! Didn't the God I believed in want us to be happy now because He loved us?"

People betray God even though they were formed by His loving hand. All too often we take upon ourselves a heavy yoke, and we live our lives in sin. But God takes pity on us. He sent His only Son to be cursed and to die and to be sacrificed and to lift the heavy yoke from off our shoulders. Through Jesus Christ, God offered us a way out from the life of sin.

For that historical work of salvation to take place in our lives, all we have to do is to believe in Jesus. Then all will be well with us and our bodies and souls will be as healthy as can be. (See 3 John 2.) This promise isn't made only to a select group of people; God prepared it for all humanity, and He made it possible for all to be saved through the cross of Jesus Christ. The salvation of the cross isn't just for the soul; it is also for the spirit, the flesh, and the present. His is a message of salvation for all. This is the Gospel of Jesus Christ. Could there be any greater love than this?

By faith, you and I were forgiven and saved by God's grace, and we were rescued from the curse, thus becoming vessels for God's blessings. By faith, we can receive healings and salvation also.

I met Jesus Christ through this hope that is grounded in faith. I discovered a pillar of fire of hope while reading God's Word during the darkest moments of my life. And subsequently I became a pastor. Through it all, I learned a poignant lesson about how important hope is.

As I kept thinking about the woman in Daejo-dong, I realized how desperately she needed this message of hope in her life. So I went back to her.

I asked, "Why don't we straighten out our fate—yours and mine?"

The woman became suspicious of what I was saying, so she asked, "What are you talking about? Why are you talking about fate? Whatever happened to the talk about Heaven? You are weird. Don't waste my time. Get out!" She continued to pour out rancorous remarks and venom, but I kept reaching out to her in spite of her words.

I said, "I know someone who can straighten out your fate. Let us go together to meet Him. He can help your husband to quit drinking, offer your children an education, and feed all of you, as well as put a solid roof over your head. Come on, let's go."

The woman finally perked up. Gradually but slowly she began to open up her heart.

Walking on the footpath between rice fields, we finally arrived at the tent church and walked inside, where old straw bags were sparsely scattered to serve as seats for the congregation.

"Where are we?" she asked.

"This is church," I said.

She glanced around the tent church and all of sudden she burst out in laughter.

Then she said, "You know what? You need to fix your fate first. We are not any different, you know. Your fate is just as pathetic as mine. What makes you think you can do something about mine?"

If you were there that day, I'm sure you would have burst out in laughter, too. But taking courage, I spoke out to her, "You're right. Our fates are lame and pathetic. But in Jesus Christ we can find hope. By placing our faith in Christ, we can be saved and be blessed materially and be set free from the curse and bondage of sin. In Him, we can receive physical healings and receive an everlasting life. What do you say? Would you like to place your faith in Him?"

Once I started talking about hope, she finally got her anger under control. From that day on, she came out to the tent church on a daily basis. We prayed and shared our hopes for the future. Amazingly, she started experiencing changes in her life. As she learned to live a life of hope, she was completely healed from her heart condition and ulcers. She then prayed for three consecutive months, asking God to heal her alcoholic husband and lead him to the church. This was a true miracle. God was at work in this woman's life.

Before long, she was able to find a job through an association of people from her hometown up north. Her life was getting better and better. Soon, her children were able to attend school; this in itself was a major miracle for this family. Furthermore, at that time people could build houses on vacant land with the consent of the landowner. So through the church we bought a small piece of land (I co-signed on the deed), and we built a house for the family with building materials that were donated to us. Her life was no longer a living hell. The woman experienced the truth that all was well with her, and she realized that her body was healthy. It was truly remarkable. I, too, was blessed by God's abundant blessings that were being poured out on her life and the realization of the message of hope, which was exemplified by her changed life.

This incident had a tremendous influence on my ministry. As a result, I boldly proclaimed the message of hope to great numbers of people and witnessed about Christ to them. The tent church grew to a 500-member church in three years. This curse- ridden village gradually became a place of hope.

The congregation prayed earnestly and lived diligently with hope filling their hearts. Pretty soon, the church was able to collect more offerings and went on to buy lands and build church buildings.

In 1961, we left the area and moved the church to Seodae-Gate area. We opened the church on a busy corner of this area, but many people ridiculed us as we did so. That's because there were some prominent churches there—Independence Door Church and A-hyun Methodist Church, as well as Jungdong Church and Saemunan Church. Many people were baffled to see a twenty-six-year-old man with no ministry experience starting a church so close to these other very eminent churches.

My thoughts were filled with God and all He would and could do through us. More precious to me than anything was the hope that I had discovered in Jesus Christ. During the 1960s South Korea experienced a monumental leap in its development. President Park Chung-Hee led the *Saemaul Movement*, which sparked the industrialization of Seoul and many job seekers flocked to the city. With no place to stay, many found a refuge in and about Ahyun-dong and Hyunjuh-dong up in the hills. People came who had no money, and they moved into the shacks I mentioned earlier.

To withstand the freezing winters, they constantly burned briquettes in order to maintain a degree of warmth in their homes. In such conditions, any slight blowing of the wind might cause the carbon monoxide gas from the burners to drift into the shacks. This was quite common in the village, and it caused the people to endure severe headaches and other harmful side effects.

It was clear to me that these residents desperately needed to hear the message of hope. I felt as if God had given me this wonderful opportunity to take His message to them. This assignment wasn't about teaching the commandments nor was it teaching about a religion. I just wanted to deliver the message of hope that is found in Jesus Christ and to let them know that it is through Him alone that salvation was readily available for them.

I remember how my simple approach was criticized harshly by many other Christian groups and pastors. However, I took hold of the reins firmly and kept sharing the message of hope more and more.

Many people flocked to the church to hear the message of hope. We began to be heavily criticized and blamed by other denominations for loudly weeping and wailing while we were in prayer. They argued that there was too much noise in a place where people need to be pious and holy. They criticized our joyful singing and clapping as we worshiped. They would say, "Frankly speaking, the middle class and the educated people don't need to cry or clap their hands during prayer and worship."

The people who came to our church had no education, money, background, or an honorable family history. Most of them were out on a limb, and they were desperate—so desperate, in fact, that they couldn't help but go to God and cry out to Him. They were crying just to live.

I stressed to them the need to cry out to God in prayer, and I told them that in the house of the Father God, they can make themselves at home and let it all out. And that's exactly what they did. The church turned into a house of mourning. During our times of worship and praise, I told them to clap in their hearts out of joy because their Father God had come to meet them. As a result, people were relieved of their stress and they were overcome with peace in their hearts. Spiritually experiencing their salvation with renewed strengthening of their faith, they also experienced physical healings. God was helping them as they went out to Him in faith and with all they had at their disposal.

It was then that I learned the most important thing in my ministry. I learned that I need to plant the very hope of God within the hearts and lives of the seekers. So even now, I go wherever they need me in an effort to plant God's hopes and dreams. In fact, I've made eighty trips around the world, and I've visited Africa, the United States, Europe, Australia, and South America. Every time I traveled I was renewed in the conviction that all people desperately desire to hear about hopes and dreams. That's because we were created in God's image—in God, where we find all our hopes and dreams. We are blessed people who can dream beautiful and precious dreams.

The renowned German theologian, Jurgen Moltmann, calls his theology "The Theology of Hope."

When Moltmann was seventeen years old, World War II broke out. He was subsequently drafted into the German Army and was dispatched to the trenches on the front lines. Eventually he became a prisoner of war. While being held captive in a British prison, he heard about the bombing of his hometown, Hamburg, and learned that his family members were all killed! Hearing this horrendous news, he fell into a major depression.

The theologian recalls this period of his life as being the worst, because he had no country and no family, and he had to deal with the neglect and abuse he experienced in the prison. On many nights he even contemplated committing suicide. In such dire straits, a pastor gave him a Bible to read. He read about Jesus being crucified on the cross and he thought about how that He, too, was rejected by His people and the world. But in spite of all that, Jesus offered goodness to people around Him and healed people along the way. However, to His dismay, the very people who received His grace stormed against Jesus and compelled Him to go to the cross. Far worse, His disciples, who should have remained close by, were the first ones to take cover when things started getting bad. Jesus died while feeling wretched and miserable, during the loneliest moments of His life. After reading the gospel accounts of Jesus' death, Moltmann began to feel strongly that he had a great deal in common with Jesus.

He read that after three days, Jesus was resurrected, and that He conquered death and the grave. Moltmann was shocked by this account of the story. Reading about the resurrection of Jesus caused him to be overcome with hope that he, too, could experience resurrection if he accepted Jesus into his heart and life. He began to think that the same thing could happen to his country and his hometown as well. It was out of these readings, thoughts, and experiences that Moltmann developed his Theology of Hope. He learned that only Jesus can offer the hope of resurrection in times of darkness and despair. Therefore, he got on his knees in the prison and accepted Jesus as his personal Savior. He realized that in Christ and in Him alone, the darkest moments of torment and despair are able to turn into light. He also learned that after the resurrection, there can no longer be darkness.

Without hopes and dreams in our hearts, no matter how well we may eat, dress, and live, we will die spiritually. On the other hand, with hopes and dreams in our hearts, we shall live, no matter how difficult our situations might be. Humans possess a strong desire to live, and hope tends to maximize that passion within us.

In I Timothy 1:1 we read, "Paul, an apostle of Jesus Christ, by the commandment of God our Savior and the Lord Jesus Christ, our hope ...." (NKJV). Paul lived with the hope that is found in Jesus Christ. In spite of adversity and hardships, Paul was able to stand firm, because he found hope through Jesus Christ. His life was filled with so much hope that even in prison he wrote letters to other Christians, encouraging them to live in joy. Even during his journey to Rome, when the ship was stranded by the wind and the waves, he boldly proclaimed the message of hope and declared God's help before others.

People usually won't share their thoughts of selfish greed and the desires of their selfish dreams with other people. But the perfect hope that is found in Christ can be shared with others, and it becomes contagious as it is shared. When hopes are shared, they become a stable foundation, which allows roots to grow and to spread. When people console each other and speak in hope, when they praise and admonish one another, the dream of hope will grow and exert a great influence on everyone.

One's future is predictable when we look at his or her dreams. Dreams are like a mirror that can give a reflection of us. This is why I proclaim the Fivefold Gospel and the Threefold Blessing to my congregation. I want to help the people cultivate their dreams through the cross. Also, I want them to treasure the dream that all is well with them and that their bodies and souls are healthy.

No matter how difficult the current circumstances of your life might be, if you possess and maintain dreams in your heart, then the dreams will take control of the third dimension and cause changes to take place within you and all around you. Dreams incubate the third-dimensional realm. No matter how void and chaotic one's life may be, if it is incubated in dreams, then changes will take place—from death to life, chaos to order, darkness to light, and poverty to abundance. I charge you, therefore, to dream in God. Preserve and hold fast to your dreams. Then you'll be in for all sorts of awesome changes in your life.

CHAPTER 5

Words

Change the Spiritual Fourth-Dimensional Realm within You

The Bible says, "Death and life are in the power of the tongue, and those who love it will eat its fruit" (Prov. 18:21, NKJV).

Words were an important element in God's work of creation. The plan of creation had been set in place, but God had to speak the words before it could become a visible reality. As such, therefore, God's words contain creativity. We have been created in His image, and we have benefited greatly from this. Our words carry creative power as well.

Of course, our words are not as perfect as God's are, but they do contain a certain amount of creative power. When we speak negatively, negative elements will manifest and grow. But if we become empowered by God and use and speak positive, creative and productive words, then their positive creative power will naturally become manifest in our lives.

In order to change our words and our language, we must first understand the importance of words. Words can hurt people as well as heal people. That's why it is imperative for us to understand the importance of words.

A single word has the power of life or death. Words are a powerful part of our lives. The Scriptures emphasize the importance of words in various passages. For example, James 3:6 says, "And the tongue is a fire, a world of iniquity. The tongue is so set among our members that it defiles the whole body, and sets on fire the course of nature; and it is set on fire by hell" (NKJV). James 3:8 says, "But no man can tame the tongue. It is an unruly evil, full of deadly poison" (NKJV). A sword may kill one person at a time, but words are much sharper and more powerful than a sword; and like an atomic bomb, they can become a weapon that can wipe out many at once.

Words Come Back Like a Boomerang

Words come back like a boomerang to the person who utters them. Spoken words not only affect one's neighbors, but they ultimately return to the person who utters them and exert an equal amount of influence on his or her life. This shows how powerful words are.

One day Leonardo da Vinci was working on an important painting. Into his studio came little children who were running around, and they caused paint to spill on the floor. He yelled out in anger immediately. The children were so shocked and scared that they left in tears. Da Vinci picked up his brush and tried to paint. But for some reason he couldn't continue painting the figure on the canvas. No matter how hard he tried, he couldn't even make his paintbrush budge. After some time had passed, it dawned on him what the problem was. He called for the children that he had scared and chased out of the room. And very politely he apologized for overreacting earlier. As a result of his apology, the children regained their smiles. After that, Da Vinci was able to continue painting.

Words tend to exert an equal amount of influence on both their speakers and their hearers, as well as anyone else who may be spoken about. The Scripture clearly points this out: "In the mouth of a fool *is* a rod of pride, but the lips of the wise will preserve them" (Prov. 14:3, NKJV). We see this in another verse from Proverbs as well: "A man will be satisfied with good by the fruit of his mouth, and the recompense of a man's hands will be rendered to him" (Prov. 12:14, NKJV).

Our Words Must Be Captivated by the Holy Spirit and the Word

Since words are powerful, they must be ruled and managed. The best instructor who can show us how to do this is the Holy Spirit. If one reacts sensitively to the leading of the Holy Spirit, then he or she will make fewer mistakes, because he or she will know what words to say under His guidance. Anytime we are speaking words that uplift and bless people, God is pleased with us and our good good language habits.

If our words can either summon curses or blessings and if we're going to be called to account before God for all the words we speak, then it is certainly wise for us to speak less. Every human being is prone to making mistakes. James 3:8 says, "But no man can tame the tongue. It is an unruly evil, full of deadly poison" (NKJV). Therefore, it is clear that the wise thing to do is to refrain from speaking, for speaking less will lead to a more peaceful and productive life.

Being able to obtain and use powerful words requires the help of the Holy Spirit, the Scriptures, and prayer. The words of God are from the fourth-dimensional realm. Words spoken with the help of the Holy Spirit are always creative, productive, and powerful, and they, likewise, will become manifest in the third-dimensional realm. That's why I want you to learn to use the spiritual language of the fourth-dimensional realm that I'm about to disclose here. If you are already using these heavenly words, I know you are already experiencing abundant blessings in your life.

1. Declare Words of Hope Aloud!

Unleash positive, *can-do* thinking through your words. Also, meditate on and memorize Scripture verses and proclaim them as if they were written for your personal life.

People often speak vain words and expressions or hear them being spoken by others. These vain words and expressions may take the form of the following: "I can't carry on any longer"; "It's too difficult for me to live this life"; or "I just can't get back on my feet anymore." Now, I don't deny the difficult reality we all live in. And it's not hard to understand why such expressions are made during difficult times. It appears as if most people are suffering with a self-inflicted "can't-do" illness, and they bind themselves up with their negative words. Therefore, these people can't accomplish much with their lives.

We might easily think, "What's the big deal about saying some useless, trivial words? They couldn't be all that bad, could they?" However, nothing could be farther from the truth. A single word that is uttered from a person's mouth has the power to either *destroy* life or *give* life to someone.

In this context, people who suffer from the "can't-do illness" can never experience creativity in their lives. God does not use people who suffer from this illness. As one speaks and holds fast to the "can't-do illness" and complains and resents God because of negative circumstances, he or she may never be able to crawl out of the pit. As a result, he or she can no longer experience the renewing of life during his or her remaining days.

Therefore, it's imperative not to speak negative words like "can't do." Don't we have our heavenly Father who created all things in the universe on our side? Don't we have His Son, our Lord Jesus Christ, who cleared up all our sins by conquering sin, illness, and all curses on the cross? Don't we have our wonderful Helper, the Holy Spirit? Then why should it be so difficult to stop speaking negative words? Why do people, even believers, continue to spit out negative words that reflect an inability to overcome sufferings and hardships? Jesus said, "If you can believe, all things are possible to him who believes" (Mark 9:23, NKJV). With His promise in mind, we must speak positive "can-do" words on a daily basis.

Many people have said to me, "Pastor Cho, how is it that you can lead a positive-spirited ministry? What is your secret to move the world?" I answer their queries by explaining about the workings of God through creative declarations.

In Spite of it All, Make Positive Declarations

At the time when Pastor Jasil Choi and I first planted the church, Korea was in an extremely poor condition. Having three meals a day was an infrequent experience for most of us. Rice was scarce, and having potatoes with our meals was a true blessing.

The number of persons in the church multiplied week after week, and the miraculous healings continued. However, our life-style didn't change much. Eventually we were able to get enough money together that enabled us to get settled into a tiny place on a hilltop. It was a two-room cubbyhole, so I took one of the rooms while Choi's family took the other.

Even though we had a place to stay, our worries about daily meals didn't go away. No one was able to offer us any help, not even the missions group at the church, which was in charge of outreach to the needy in the local area. On certain nights, we had only sweet potatoes for supper. We would split these sweet potatoes among the five of us and would fill up our stomachs with tap water. On such nights, no one said much. We just went to bed and tried to go to sleep. Our lay minister, Choi, was our anchor, and she would pray late into the night in her room, then leave for church early in the morning so she could pray in tongues and beseech God. You can only survive on sweet potatoes for so long, and trying to do so was becoming almost unbearable. Nonetheless, we had to stave off the continual hunger that we experienced every day.

One morning, I became overwhelmed with what I like to describe as explosive faith in my heart. I felt it was the Holy Spirit, and I believed He wanted to use me as a mouthpiece for proclaiming His message. I stood in front of a mirror. With both of my fists clenched, I began to shout, as I stared fiercely at myself.

"Yonggi Cho, you are not poor!"

"Yonggi Cho, you are wealthy!"

"Our church shall reach 1,000 members by next year!"

"Yonggi Cho, you suffered from tuberculosis in the past, but look at you now; you are healthy!"

"Yonggi Cho, you have the faith to move a mountain. Whoever believes can achieve anything!"

As I uttered these faith-filled declarations, I sensed I wasn't alone. When I opened the door, I found lay minister Choi standing there. I couldn't look her in the eye, because I felt pitiful, embarrassed, and awkward. Even so, I kept using positive words that helped me to encourage myself and kept on repeating them over and over again.

As I maintained that spirit, God started moving in my life and subsequently I was able to plant the world's largest church with the help of God and His blessings. However, if I had just dwelt on the negative developments of life and the church in those days, I would have remained a failure forever, always saying and repeating words like, "I can't do it"; "It can't be done"; and "It's not possible."

Anymore, before I go to bed, I proclaim, "I can do it. I'm a blessed man in Christ Jesus. I'm successful." When I wake up in the morning, I cry out, "I can be successful because God has empowered me." Of course, I say this in full faith that God will pour out His power through my positive and creative declarations, and He will use me to do great things.

It's time for you to change your words. Remove these words and negative declarations from your vocabulary: "I just can't do this—I just can't!" and get rid of all negative words. Instead, fill your mouth with positive words by saying, "I can do it. No matter what anyone says, I can get back on my feet again." In this way, you can break free from all restraints and change your life for the better by filling your life with positive, productive, and creative words. As you move forward in God, He will pour out His power and blessings and enable you to do miraculous things; the dire circumstances of your life will turn into a new environment, one that is full of fulfilled promises. As a result, your life will change drastically and your nation and fellow-citizens will start to change as well.

2. Release Your Faith Through Words.

Words are essential tools that are needed to engage in spiritual warfare and to overcome all dire circumstances. So release your faith through words. Claim and reclaim God's promises over and over again with your mouth. In so doing, you shall experience awesome changes.

Reverend Stanley Jones is well known for his missionary work in India and also for his positive beliefs. He was a writer, missionary, and messenger of the gospel. He had lived a healthy life with a positive outlook and mind-set, but when he approached the age of 89, a stroke set him back. He was bedridden for a long time and was unable to speak. He asked his nurse for a favor: "Please claim in words, 'In the name of

Jesus, you shall walk,' night and day." Since he was completely paralyzed, he asked the nurse to do this in his behalf. From then on, his nurses always proclaimed those words, and Reverend Jones always responded, "Amen!"

People who knew about this would laugh at him. But Reverend Jones was someone who knew about the power that exists in words. Before he was fully healed, he made a trip to an area in the Himalayas for some rest. While he was there, he asked the nurses to proclaim those same positive words in his behalf. After some time passed, this eighty-nine-year-old man who had been suffering from a stroke was completely healed! The power for healing came from the words that were proclaimed by mouth. In other words, he released his faith through words, and he changed his third-dimensional circumstances with a fourth-dimensional element: *words*.

Miracles are possible when we use our words to proclaim that God will respond to our dreams and our faith. And as we share that faith with others, those very words become the light that eradicates darkness, that bring life out of death, and that cause something to exist out of nothing. How important it is to dream, to pray in faith, and to proclaim your dreams and faith by the words of your mouth! When we proclaim our faith through the words we utter, we release our faith, which is the power that will bring about awesome and creative changes.

Confess Your Faith with Your Mouth

We must confess our salvation with our mouths. Romans 10:9-10 says "that if you confess with your mouth the Lord Jesus and believe in your heart that God has raised Him from the dead, you will be saved. For with the heart one believes unto righteousness, and with the mouth confession is made unto salvation" (NKJV). No matter how much faith we have in Jesus, if we keep it in our hearts and do not confess it with our mouths, we can't receive His salvation. You must say, "I believe in Jesus as my Lord and Savior." This is because the words we speak provide the creative context in which God's workings become manifest.

Matthew 10:32-33 says, "Therefore whoever confesses Me before men, him I will also confess before My Father who is in heaven. But whoever denies Me before men, him I will also deny before My Father who is in heaven" (NKJV). Confessing and denying are both done with the mouth. We must come to know and acknowledge that the power of life or death resides in our tongues.

This is a good place to share the personal testimony of one member of my congregation. Her name is Ms. Jung Yoo-sun, and she suffered a physical collapse a few years back. She thought she had been suffering from a common cold, but what it turned out to be was something far more serious. One day she fainted after her heartbeat became irregular. Then she fell into a coma.

When she regained her consciousness after nine days, she awoke to learn that she had been diagnosed with terminal cancer in her lymphatic glands. She was devastated by this news. From that point on, she cried out to God and asked Him to spare her life. She prayed, "If you spare my life, I'll live the rest of my life for you." She began chemotherapy, but her condition worsened and the doctor called in her family to prepare for her funeral. In spite of this, Ms. Jung never gave up. She wasn't about to let go of her faith in God.

She bought tapes of sermons and kept listening to them in the hospital room. She was inspired by one sermon in particular, which proclaimed the following message: "Where is your sting, O death? You can't win, O death!" She took hold of that saying and felt as if those words were penetrating deep into her heart. From then on, she kept confessing the same words, and as she did so, she kept on confronting and fighting death. She would repeat these words over and over again: "Where is your sting, O death? Death, you can't win! I'm healed by Jesus. His precious blood has cleansed me! Depart from me, O death!"

Every time she would receive an injection from the nurses, she would proclaim by mouth, "Jesus was beaten so that I would be healed! I am healed!" A few days later she attended a grand gathering at the church and received the laying on of hands and my prayers. She later shared that at that moment she felt something moving through her body; it was the healing work of the Holy Spirit. She then returned to the hospital for a checkup. To everyone's surprise, there was no cancer found in her body! Even the doctors called it a miracle. Eventually, through this incident, her unbelieving husband and her in-laws came to know the Lord.

The power of one's confession by mouth is amazing. This is what sets apart believers from nonbelievers and enables believers to confront death. Nonbelievers have no weapons with which to fight death. But we have a powerful weapon at our disposa—the Word of God! The Word is the sword of the Spirit. Once we accept God's will and God's Word into our hearts and confess them by our mouths in faith, we shall gain the victory.

Command in Faith

During a time of long and serious prayer, one may feel a conviction in his or her heart that his or her prayers have already been answered. When this happens, you must claim it as if the invisible has become visible.

For example, you might pray, "Father God, I want to thank you in advance for healing me. I'm completely healed. You've already cleansed me from my illness. My non-believing family has already received their salvation, so reach out to them."

After that, there is something else that must be done. Once you feel that firm belief and conviction in your heart and feel certain that you can claim the invisible as visible, then it is time to command the "mountain" that looms in front of you and tell it what it must do:

"Be gone, O great big mountain!"

"Be gone, O illness!"

"Be gone, O unbelief!"

"Be gone, O curse!"

"Be gone, O poverty!"

The time to witness the miracle is when you make the command. God said, "Let there be light," and there was light. He then commanded, "Let there be a firmament," and a firmament appeared. He said, "Let the waters under the heavens be gathered together into one place," and dry land appeared. He then said, "Let the earth bring forth grass, the herb that yields seed, and the fruit tree that yields fruit according to its kind," and it was so. (See Gen. 1.)

Jesus always performed the miracles when He commanded them. For example, He said, "You have been forgiven"; "Now, pick up your mat and go"; "Depart, O evil spirit"; and "Lazarus, come out." Each time when He issued a command, a miracle followed immediately.

Commands always precede the creative workings of God; these things don't happen through begging on bended knees or cries of desperation. So, once you believe and can proclaim the invisible as being visible, then shout out your commands:

"Depart from me, O illness!"

"My family shall return to the Lord in hurry!"

"Appear, O job!"

"Draw near, O blessings!"

There might be differences from person to person with regard to the time that passes between something that is believed and its visible manifestation, but someone who disregards the time factor and transcends time by believing in his or her heart and making confession by word of mouth, shall then receive that which he or she seeks.

We must remember that we are engaged in a spiritual warfare every day and every moment. First Peter 5:8-9 says, "Be sober, be vigilant; because your adversary the devil walks about like a roaring lion, seeking whom he may devour. Resist him, steadfast in the faith, knowing that the same sufferings are experienced by your brotherhood in the world" (NKJV).

Yes, the devil is always roaming around and seeking to devour us with every means and method that he has at his disposal. So we must be very careful not to fall into his traps. We have our Lord Jesus Christ by our side, and He paid the dear price of sin with His innocent bloodshed. There are no reasons to give up or step down. From now on, let's proclaim the words of our Lord and confess them with our mouths and be victorious in all spiritual battles.

3. Speak Creative and Successful Words

Words can either kill or bring someone to life. Let us strive to say only words of inspiration, the creative words that summon success and joy.

Even when we utter a single word, we must make sure it is a creative word that offers inspiration, joy, and success. Words have the power to bring into existence what they say.

An inspirational speaker, trainer, and teacher of passionate living and the positive mind-set, Dr. Zig Ziglar, was in New York City and was about to get on the subway when he saw a beggar who was selling pencils for a dollar apiece. Dr. Ziglar had sympathy for the beggar, so he pulled out a dollar bill and dropped it in his box, unconcerned about getting the pencil the man was offering. As he walked away, however, he decided to turn around and go back to the beggar.

He said, "I want my pencil for the dollar I dropped into the box."

The beggar gave him a pencil. As he received his pencil, Dr. Ziglar said, "You are a businessman like me. You are no longer a beggar."

As a result of hearing those words, the beggar's life turned around completely. Dr. Ziglar had called him a businessman, not a beggar. He was a businessman who was trying to make a living by selling pencils. That man eventually went on to become a successful businessman. He was able to do so because his self-portrait had completely changed. He was deeply encouraged by hearing the word "businessman" associated with himself.

On his way home, he began to mutter these words, "I'm not a beggar. I'm a businessman—a businessman who sells pencils."

His dreams, his self-portrait and his faith had changed, and, as a result, this man became a successful businessman. Some time later, he went to see Dr. Ziglar. He said, "Your words changed my life completely. Most people just drop a dollar bill in my basket and walk away. They're completely indifferent about the pencils, so I thought that that was all there was to it. I always thought of myself as a beggar, but that day when you came to me, you called me 'a businessman' just like you. Those words changed my life forever."

Words that come out of our mouths can change another person's life completely. What's even more interesting is that words can affect even the water we drink. A Japanese expert on wave and motion, Emodo Masaro, wrote a book entitled, *Water Contains the Answer*, in which he shows how water reacts to love.

Masaro argues that if humans speak contemptuous words to a glass of drinking water, the shapes of the crystals in the water molecules will break apart, leaving ugly shapes in place of the former ones. If someone wrote the word *evil* on the crystals of water molecules, an ugly hole would be formed. He also observed that if we thank the water that we're about to drink, then the crystals of the water molecules become six-sided. Furthermore, if we say, "I love you," the crystals take on very beautiful shapes. That's because the message of love is communicated through some unknown frequency and somehow it is able to affect even water molecules.

Therefore, even water gains vitality when it is loved. What's interesting about this is that the human body is composed of sixty percent water. So when we express contempt, anger, and cursing to others, the crystals of water molecules inside their bodies and ours, as well, will get seriously distorted, and ultimately this will lead to diseases and illnesses. If we share love and encouragement instead, the water molecules will react accordingly and become six-sided crystalline figures, providing us with vitality and a healthy life.

This tells us that speaking out of love is closely related to our life and our health, and such loving words can even improve the quality of our lives and health. Therefore, let's be sure to use words that offer life.

A righteous person should always think deeply about the words that should be used and when and where to use them. He or she should also speak only words of wisdom and love, words that offer life to others. The tongue of a righteous person is as valuable as silver of the highest quality because it has no impurities. And the listeners to the words of such a righteous person will be led to the path of life. Remember, our words always yield results.

4. Always Speak Words that are Filtered by Heavenly Language!

Words that contain love and blessings can change people and turn any place into a blessed environment. If you speak words out of love, which is the heavenly language, then the Holy Spirit will perform miracles through your tongue.

The kind of language teenagers use these days may seem like a foreign language to many of us. In South Korea, for example, teenagers have coined new words and codes from existing words, and they use them like a new language. These adaptations and variations make it difficult for someone like me to comprehend what they're saying to each other. What's even worse is the language and signs that are used in on-line chat rooms and during text messaging. Most of these systems of communication use codes, acronyms, and abbreviations that I don't understand. It's not difficult for young people to understand these things though, because it's a language of their own.

Words of Love and Blessings

Like the secret language teenagers use, citizens of Heaven have an exclusive language of their own as well. And we must use it because it marks our true identity; it's a sign that confirms our changed identity. The words of our language may well be incomprehensible to non-believers. But those who believe in Jesus Christ understand them. As long as we claim to be people of faith, we must know how to speak the heavenly tongue. That's because by speaking and using our heavenly language, we are able to live according to heavenly means. Because our tongues rule over our bodies, our bodies and lives will change according to what we speak.

Words that contain love and blessings really do change people, and they make the environment more blessed. Therefore, we should never speak words that reflect dissatisfaction nor utter complaints or profanity, no matter what the circumstances are. During difficult times, we should use our heavenly language, the words of blessing and love, because when we do, we allow the Holy Spirit to make use of our tongues.

The words that come out of our mouths create and form our lives. This is like a silkworm using its silk to make a cocoon for itself. The uttered proclamations from our mouths structure and create the environment in which we live. That's why we must take caution when we speak. When the Holy Spirit comes upon us, we become empowered by Him and thus we speak in tongues. This is a surprise to people sometimes, because speaking in tongues comes from the leading of the Holy Spirit. Therefore, we must become Christians who speak in heavenly tongues that are guided by the Holy Spirit.

Words of Gratitude, Words that Confess Our Faith

If we live our lives in constant bickering and lamenting, our lives will self-destruct. The Scripture says, "He replied, 'I tell you that to everyone who has, more will be given, but as for the one who has nothing, even what he has will be taken away'" (Luke 19:26, NIV). If we confess with our mouths that what we desire doesn't exist, God will take away even what does exist. But if we think about what we have and give thanks to God, He will bless us with even better things.

Psalm 22:3 says, "But You are holy, enthroned in the praises of Israel" (NKJV). Once God is enthroned, then all hardships will vanish, and only the victory will remain. That's why the Scripture tells us to always give thanks. God inhabits our praises.

One important point about the power of the words we utter is the fact that those very words can become actual realities in our lives. Therefore, claim your dreams boldly. Look to the cross and boldly welcome the dreams of the gospel and a life that is full of blessings. Declare your confessions of faith in positive ways. The following are some affirmations and declarations that you will want to make often:

"I was declared righteous when I received the forgiveness of Jesus."

"Because of Jesus, the devil will depart from me, and Heaven and the Holy Spirit will take his place."

"By God's mercy and grace, the illness of my heart is healed, and my physical illnesses have been removed from me."

We must always believe that our lives, through the blessings of God's salvation and the message of the gospel, will always be renewed, as we live and rest near the green pasture and waterside God has provided for us (see Ps. 23.); and that once we change this faith into reality, we'll be able to live lives that are filled with abundant blessings.

Proclaim your faith in words, and take action. We'll gain strength once we realize that Jesus Christ has already taken our yoke upon himself, and He has prayed for us. He has provided righteousness and goodness for us through the promises He made by His blood on the cross. To overcome our circumstances, we must claim His promises and speak them forth.

The sufferings and trials we go through in life are God's way of preparing us to be vessels that contain His blessings. The sufferings we may be going through now will someday become rewards.

Words are the closest thing—our connection—to the reality of God's fourth-dimensional realm. Words, more than any other element, reflect this reality. Through the words we utter, we will be able to get a glimpse into God's fourth-dimensional realm and receive His faith and His dreams. That's why I've reserved the discussion of words to be the last of all the fourth-dimensional elements.

Proverbs 6:2 says, "You are snared by the words of your mouth; you are taken by the words of your mouth" (NKJV).

We shall be held accountable before God for every word we've ever spoken. Therefore, every single word you utter counts for eternity.

Jesus said, "For David himself said by the Holy Spirit: 'The LORD said to my Lord, Sit at My right hand, till I make Your enemies Your footstool.' Therefore David himself calls Him '*Lord*'; how is He then his Son?" And the common people heard Him gladly (Mark 12:36-37, NKJV).

God will use words as a ruler of measurement for separating the righteous from the unrighteous on Judgment Day. God knows everything we have ever said, and He will remember all that we've ever uttered from our mouths and the thoughts that were in our hearts and minds as well. Therefore, we must plant ourselves on the foundation of the Scriptures and use the words of the Bible as the foundation for our own words. When we use creative words that are based on faith, we will experience amazing changes in our lives.

CHAPTER 6

Epilogue

Meet God in Your Spiritual Training, as You Train Yourself in Fourth-Dimensional Spirituality

The Bible says, "For we do not wrestle against flesh and blood, but against principalities, against powers, against the rulers of the darkness of this age, against spiritual hosts of wickedness in the heavenly places" (Eph. 6:12, NKJV).

So far, we have examined fourth-dimensional spirituality and its four elements—thinking, faith, dreams, and words—the components that rule our third-dimensional lives. How is your fourth-dimensional spiritual realm right now?

Were you encouraged to apply the spiritual changes I've outlined in this book to your own life? Or do you find it too difficult to take on these challenges even though you can now understand these concepts? Perhaps you are thinking, I'm happy with the way I am now; it's not necessary for me to change anything. The world is changing quite rapidly, however, and the truth of the matter is that your life is constantly and continually being challenged from every direction. You may not want to be bothered by these elements of change, but you need to be aware that Satan and his principalities are continually unleashing their attacks and the forces of evil are opposing you even now.

Whenever a person is going through struggles and trials, he or she is likely to ask, "Why am I suffering like this?" That person might say, "I don't see others suffering the way I am, so why me? Why is my life filled with these problems?" Such challenging moments in life prompt us to react and come up with means and measures to confront them. God has ways and means to help you if you will avail yourself of them.

A few years back, when I was ministering at a major spiritual gathering in the Philippines, I was invited to visit the president of the Philippines.

During our chat, the president said, "Pastor Cho, we have a big problem. With the massive influx of western influence into our country, our younger generation is becoming morally corrupt. Whatever the government tries to do is done in vain. Presently, we've created some temporary measures, such as promoting sports-related activities to lead them to become sounder in their minds and bodies."

I responded, "Sports might train their physical bodies, but they cannot change their hearts completely. The only thing that can change them within is the power of the blood of our resurrected Lord Jesus Christ and the power of the Holy Spirit. For young Filipinos to become morally sound, they must arm themselves with faith in Jesus and become anointed by the Holy Spirit. So, Mr. President, you must start a spiritual revival movement."

Getting rid of the spider webs in the house isn't going to remove the infestation; unless one gets to the root of the problem, the house will continue to have spider webs and spiders. Likewise, no matter how hard a society may try to deal with crime and its perpetrators by writing more laws or establishing more stringent policies, unless there are fundamental changes within the hearts of people, it will all be in vain. The approach to the problem has to be different; it must be a spiritual approach. People's hearts don't move unless they're inspired. So the crux of the matter is to know what to do with the human heart.

Confront Your Problems with Fourth-Dimensional Spirituality!

People who possess spiritual discernment deal with their problems differently than other people do. Take a look at the story of Joseph being sold to Egypt by his older brothers, for example. Examining Joseph's life and circumstances after he was sold into slavery from a third-dimensional perspective would reveal that his life was in a state of complete chaos – a most unfortunate, sad, and horrible set of circumstances.

But how did Joseph see his situation, and how did he deal with his circumstances? Had he approached his situation from a third-dimensional perspective, he would have been filled with a burning passion for revenge. But Joseph possessed the spiritual discernment he needed to deal with his problems and circumstances in a different way. He looked at things from the fourth-dimensional point of view, and this enabled him to see that what was taking place in his life was the work of God, which was taking place to bless and save his life.

Likewise, if we deal with problems that are incurred from the third-dimensional realm with a third-dimensional approach, then our situations will get worse and we will see no resolutions for our problems. If we rely only on the knowledge we gain from our physical senses in the third-dimensional realm of our Christian walk, then we are bound to have continuing problems. If we approach our problems by tapping into our fleshly passions, insights, boasting, reason, experience, and the knowledge we've gained from the third-dimensional realm, we will be starting off on the wrong foot, and we will be seriously defeated by the darkness of this age and its rulers. .

To gain knowledge of the fourth-dimensional realm, we must tap into the Word of God and the guidance of the Holy Spirit. We will fall prey to the perils of life and be devoured by Satan if we rely on ourselves and our human ways to deal with life's problems. That's because this world is in the third-dimensional realm, and to be victorious in this realm, we must rely on the tools and offensive weapons of the fourth-dimensional realm. Basically, our approach to dealing with the problems of life should be different from the world's way of dealing with problems. How we decide to understand and deal with the issues of life and the problems that originate from the third-dimensional realm will affect how we look at life in the third-dimensional realm. The answer lies in changing our fourth-dimensional realm. Once that spiritual part of us has been changed, we will be able to control life in the third-dimensional realm.

Therefore, as you can see, fourth-dimensional spirituality is a blessing from God. We must change the four elements of the fourth-dimensional realm—our thinking, faith, dreaming, and words—so that our third-dimensional realm will become a life full of blessings.

Non-believers, too, can achieve their goals in the third-dimensional realm by working hard and possessing positive thinking and using words of belief. These fourth-dimensional elements are universal laws of nature. However, powerful changes and miracles can only occur when we employ God's ways through prayer, meditation on the Word, and the help of the Holy Spirit as born-again believers.

Throughout this book we've looked at the specifics of change and how spiritual principles are to be applied. I trust that you've begun to put some of these principles to work in your own life as you've been reading. But let me remind you that it's more important to be persistent in your practice of these principles and not be finished with them after one or two tries. I hope and pray that fourth-dimensional spirituality will occupy the center stage in your life. I hope and pray that these truths and principles will become your very own spiritual habits. Of course, that's easier said than done, but don't give up, and be sure to keep on challenging yourself. You will be able to, as the Holy Spirit leads you and helps you.

Changing One's Fourth-Dimensional Realm Involves Spiritual Warfare

Humans are weak and timid beings. Human strength alone can't change the terrain that leads to the fourth-dimensional realm. Even if you desperately try to think positively, for instance, you can easily get fooled by your own feelings and emotions. To maintain positive emotions for a prolonged period of time is not an easy task. Also, there are external factors that happen in our world and we can't ignore them. No matter how hard we try to change, due to temptations from the world and Satan's persistent attacks, it is likely that we might give up or fail completely. This is because changing the fourth-dimensional realm always affects the spiritual realm around us, and the darkness of this age and spiritual hosts of wickedness will try to thwart our efforts. Be assured that this is truly a matter of spiritual warfare.

Paul writes, "For we do not wrestle against flesh and blood, but against principalities, against powers, against the rulers of the darkness of this age, against spiritual hosts of wickedness in the heavenly places" (Eph. 6:12, NKJV).

This brings us to a stark reality: Our life issues and problems are spiritual issues and problems. In this struggle, however, we will ultimately be able to taste victory. To prepare ourselves for the battle, we must be trained. Spiritual training is absolutely imperative. If we make God the Lord of our lives, changing the four elements of the fourth-dimensional realm according to the will of God is feasible through spiritual training and discipline. There are three steps in this spiritual training process: training in prayer, training in the Word, and training in the Holy Spirit.

Training in Prayer

First and foremost, we need to be trained in prayer. The work of the Holy Spirit cannot occur within us without prayer backing it up. And without the Holy Spirit, we'll never get *spirituality* right. The development of spirituality within us takes place through prayer. Therefore, training in prayer is absolutely imperative. I try to make every effort to give prayer my undivided attention every day. Prayer, to me, is life itself. Let's take a brief look at this important topic.

First, we have what I call *prayer journaling*.Through this means,I keep a record of my prayer life—what I'm praying for and how God answers my prayers. In prayer, I plan my daily activities and I establish my goals for the future. Before I start each new day,I lift up my prayers to the throne of God.I pray throughout the day to gain victory on a moment-to-moment basis, and I conclude my day with prayer as well.

Second, I use *pre-working prayer* before I start my ministerial work or preach from the pulpit. I see prayer as being a ministry toward an invisible God. I often tell my students,"Before you minister to people,minister to God first." Before beginning the ministry of proclaiming the Word of God from the pulpit, God must be ministered to through prayer.

Third is the *prayer of faith*.I want to stress the importance of praying in faith, without any doubt whatsoever.To engage in the prayer in faith, you must trust implicitly in God, and the goals of your prayers must be clear. Confess everything in positive faith, and anticipate God's miracles.Also, learn the law of meditation in faith.

Fourth is the *prayer of command*. Prayer in faith must stand on declared faith. This is similar to using the power that was bestowed on Christ. To subdue the creation around us and to be the conduits through which miracles can flow, we must pray in commanding faith by declaring what we want and believe.

Fifth is the *prayer of community*. I'd like to stress the importance of what I call fasting prayers and crying-aloud prayers.To engage in prayer while fasting forfeits drinking and eating and desires God with all our hearts,as we seek His grace and mercy to help us in our time of need. (See Heb. 4:16.)

Crying-aloud prayers lengthen our time of concentration, and these kinds of prayer are very effective in our spiritual training, because they provide us with a powerful means to call upon God's strength, mercy, and grace. These prayers can also be effective in creating unity among the members of the believing community, including the leaders, enabling the body of believers to create a praying culture.

Besides the things I've just mentioned, there are many other forms and models of prayer. We've already discussed some effective prayers that can be used to enable us to feel the presence of our Lord and to withstand the evil influences in our lives. You will discover how grand and expansive prayer can be through our Lord's Prayer, worship, praise, and the prayer of spiritual discernment. I'd also like to stress the importance of praying in tongues. Once we begin to pray in tongues through the anointing of the Holy Spirit and the inner workings of our hearts, we'll be able to transcend all timidity, weakness, and fear, and experience God's awesome presence and grace much more deeply.

Through prayer we are empowered by the Holy Spirit in our fourth-dimensional realm, and this changes the way we think, dream, have faith, and speak.

Training in the Word

The Word of God contains the will and thoughts of God. Our new thinking, appearance, and language are completed through the spiritual Word of our living God. Meditating upon and memorizing Scriptures develops and improves our fourth-dimensional realm. Members of a church's congregation experience the fourth-dimensional realm as they hear their pastor's messages. Therefore, the direction of the lives of Christians can change for the better as each of us becomes sensitive to and tunes into God's Word.

Also, the Word of God must be experienced in our daily lives. Even though the Bible is the inspired Word of God, unless we experience God's power and His works in our daily lives, the Scriptures will be meaningless to us. During every Lord's Day worship service, I recite twenty different verses from the Scriptures. And I exhort the members of the congregation to study, memorize, and apply the Word of God in their lives each day. I believe that our thinking, faith, dreams, and words must be inspired by the will of God and His Word. I hope and pray that your fourth-dimensional spirituality is growing as you understand, meditate upon, and memorize the Scriptures.

Training in the Holy Spirit

Each one of us needs the training that is provided by, in, and through the Holy Spirit. Therefore, you need to focus on the following three things and experience them in your life:

First, stay in communion with the Holy Spirit. In the earlier years of my ministry, I didn't know much about the Person of the Holy Spirit. After an early morning prayer service one day in 1964, I heard the voice of the Holy Spirit while I was praying for the revival of the church. He said, "*You know Me only through your personal encounters, but I'm a Person. Beings with a personality can't be known only through occasional encounters; they come to be known through fellowship and personal experience. Therefore, you must express gratitude for Me, welcome Me, and acknowledge Me as a Person.*" From that day on, I began conversing deeply with the Holy Spirit, and I started experiencing God's amazing grace in my life.

Second, we must learn to work with the Holy Spirit as His companion. Communion with the Holy Spirit is manifested by the power and the works of Almighty God. Success or failure in our lives is determined by how much we accept Him as our Companion and Helper in our ministries.

Third, we must be in unity with the Holy Spirit. Unity with the Holy Spirit means being in a personal relationship with Him, being His companion, and being one with Him in the fullest measure of oneness. Unity with the Holy Spirit will lead you into a life that is truly filled with the Holy Spirit.

When we are filled with the Holy Spirit, our dreams can be achieved. We can dream to become the witnesses of Christ instead of dreaming selfish dreams and living selfishly. The Holy Spirit can touch and move us from the three-dimensional realm and lead us to the realm of the fourth dimension where creative changes in our lives are waiting for us.

Anticipate God's Miracles and Experience Them in Your Life

The spiritual realm of the fourth dimension is the roadway where God's children and God's workings merge together. Also, through fourth-dimensional spirituality, you will be able to experience great changes in your third-dimensional realm. You can change your thinking, your level of faith, your dreams, and your words through prayer and the Word. The Holy Spirit will guide and help you to change your life and to live your life in a way that fulfills the mission that Christ has ordained for you.

Through fourth-dimensional spirituality I received visions from the Holy Spirit. This spiritual experience combined with faith brought me into new realms of spiritual authority, and it made it possible for Yoido Full Gospel Church to grow and expand through God's power. I've experienced many miracles throughout my ministry, and I've come to realize that miracles are exclusively within God's realm and they are subject to His sovereignty. Miracles are continuing to be manifested in our church today. We're seeing changed lives, the resolutions of all kinds of problems, healings, etc. Such phenomena are becoming almost natural to our congregation. This happens because we believe that God, who transcends all things, is active in our midst, and He is interceding in our lives to help us deal with life's problems.

So, no matter what difficult circumstances might loom before you today, start dreaming of victory. Believe the promises of God. Speak declarations of faith. Lean on the power of the Holy Spirit.

We have special privileges through the grace of our Lord Jesus Christ. We can dream life instead of death, victory instead of defeat, health instead of illness, and success instead of failure. Hold fast to our Lord's promise: "I am the LORD your God, who brought you out of the land of Egypt; open your mouth wide, and I will fill it" (Ps. 81:10, NKJV), and dream big. Dreaming is the *word* of the Holy Spirit, and to dream means you are walking together with the Holy Spirit. You can claim victory as you proclaim your dream in words without ceasing and as you engage in affirmative, positive, and creative dreams and thinking.

Declare spiritual victory over your life right now. Confront the problems of your life with thinking, faith, dreams, and words of fourth-dimensional spirituality from now on. And continue to yearn for the training you need to experience victory in spiritual warfare. Through training in prayer, training in the Word, and training in the Holy Spirit, your fourth-dimension spirituality will become a sanctified habit, not a one-time spiritual high. And you will experience continual change within your life. You will experience great and awesome miracles, and you will become a believer who is on a mission to achieve God's dreams. It is with my exhortation and supplication that I pray that your life will be filled with God's amazing grace and blessings, and that His works will be manifested through His supernatural miracles.

Yes, fourth-dimensional spirituality is entirely possible for you to experience in your three-dimensional world!